MARKETWISE

MarketWise

VICTORIA M. RYCE

Stoddart

First published in 1988 by
Stoddart Publishing Co. Limited
34 Lesmill Road
Toronto, Canada
M3B 2T6

Canadian Cataloguing in Publication Data

Marketwise
 Victoria M. Ryce

ISBN 0-7737-5143-2

1. Investments. 2. Stock-exchange. 3. Finance, Personal. I. Title.

HG4521.R92 1988   332.6'78   C88-093699-1

Line drawings: Anthony A. Gower
Jacket design: Falcom Design & Communications
Typesetting: Jay Tee Graphics Ltd.
Printed and bound in Canada

This book is dedicated to
My father, who gave me my determination
My mother, from whom I inherited creative skills, and
My brother, whom I am determined will be Marketwise!

ACKNOWLEDGEMENTS

I sincerely appreciate the help everyone has given me with this book. First, my right hand on this project, Liss Jeffrey, who produced this book with the utmost efficiency, professionalism, and talent. I am forever grateful to you, Liss, for your superb contribution.

Second, I thank all my clients and those who attended my investment courses for improving my understanding of investments and allowing me to help other people understand them better.

To everyone who read parts of this book in manuscript and made helpful suggestions, I know this book is substantially improved because of your input. Thank you, John Paul Campbell, Peter Heyerdahl, Linda Jackson, David Louis, Jean and Bas Allen, Stephen Ross, Daniel McCarthy, Robert Black, and James W. Moir, Jr.

Many people helped shape my investment thinking over the years, especially people at Moss, Lawson & Co. Limited, Burns Fry Limited, and Merrill Lynch Canada Inc. In particular, I would like to acknowledge Merrill Lynch Canada Inc. for the kind permission to use many of its documents.

I am grateful to Naomi Ridout, who helped me obtain my first job in the industry; Steven Kelman, who gave me my first paying assignment to write an investment article; and Alan Silverstein, who brought Stoddart Publishing and me together. Betty Lee, thanks for your insight and especially for bringing Liss and me together. Where Liss left off, Lenore d'Anjou took over and edited me across the finish line. Thanks.

Michael Taylor, thank you for holding my hand and critiquing the entire manuscript twice over its lifetime.

The person who always told me I could make it in the investment world is my close friend, Jacqueline O. Reimer. J, your encouragement and love have been a continuous source of joy in my life. I thank you for reading my book, liking it, and believing in me.

Finally, to Norman Harold Ringel, who likes to be known as Normy. I thank you for constantly putting an effort into this book from the original idea to the final copy. You know what I'm trying to say.

To family, friends, and business associates, cheers!

CONTENTS

INTRODUCTION

Welcome to the world of investments. This book contains thousands of dollars of practical advice for you. I have written for you — a person looking for an action-oriented guide — to help you leapfrog your investment knowledge above that of the crowd. If your goal is to develop investment intelligence and confidence in order to make decisions resulting in the best use of your money, you've come to the right place.

Not only will I help you learn to converse with ease about the stock market. I will also give you practical, helpful, and action-oriented steps which will make *you* a better investor. Here are concrete suggestions and tools to use in the investment world.

Maybe you have been an investor before, or maybe this is your first attempt to profit from the investment activity in the market. Either way, this book can help you.

I will provide you with step-by-step instructions on where to find information, understand it, and then benefit from using it.

One of the biggest hurdles potential investors face is the overwhelming amount of available information. Where do you begin? As John Naisbitt says in his bestselling *Megatrends*, "We are drowning in information, but starved for knowledge." It is exactly this knowledge or know-how that you will find here in manageable, bite-size pieces. I will take you one step at a time through the investment world and pass on the information you need to benefit from investing. By eliminating the information you don't really need, I have been able to keep explanations of the investment process streamlined and to the point. You don't want to waste time.

What is your goal? You want to be someone who understands the language, the ideas, and the actions needed to operate in the investment world. If you don't know what a "round turn" is, you aren't without intelligence, you just lack specific training in the land of investor lingo. (A round turn is simply the commission charged when you complete both sides of a future transaction. Easy, once it is explained to you.)

We will explore Bay Street, Wall Street, and the world. Why? To see what is available for you in Canada, in North America, and around the globe. Today's investors are virtually unlimited in their choice of products and places to invest. You will become familiar with where the action happens and why.

You will find many true stories in this book about how other people have invested. The names have been changed to protect the rich and the poor, the innocent and the guilty, (and the just embarrassed), but I think that you will find their experiences helpful in your journey to become a marketwise investor.

Do you need to be older to be a better investor? It helps. Do you need experience? It helps. But if you are young and you don't have stock market experience, don't despair. Young or old, you can still learn to be a better investor by reading this book. I can't promise you beginner's luck, but I do know that the sooner you start learning about investing, the faster you are going to become attuned to the workings of the market.

Go and get a pen or pencil. I know that you will derive the greatest benefit from this book if you write in it, filling in the various checklists, highlighting points which are of particular importance to you, and personalizing wherever possible. This book could be the key to your financial freedom so use it as a workbook, a progress report, and an information source. *Don't let this book sit on your shelf.* I wrote it so that you can benefit from the world of investment opportunities. Use it!

I have put into perspective some old and wise ideas and strategies. You can learn valuable lessons from investors who've gone before you. For this reason I will recommend some books which were written many years ago. Some investment ideas and mottos never change, regardless of what happens. *Buy low and sell high* is probably the world's most famous example.

To prepare you to enter the financial marketplace, I have organized this book to start with discovering your present situation, your goals, and your strategies for reaching them. This is an important step before we discuss specific investment vehicles. Later we'll move to details about various kinds of investment choices; you can examine them at close range to determine if they suit your needs. Along the way, we will put all of this learning into perspective by slotting it into a personal master plan which you will develop here.

I strongly believe evidence that you can make a great deal of money in the stock market. Historical and statistical facts provide proof. I am not naïve. I don't think that everybody makes money in the stock market. Sometimes it's not the individual's fault. But I do know that some people don't make money there because they made mistakes that could easily have been corrected. I'll show you how to spot the traps and avoid them. This is one of your main goals when investing: to avoid stepping into investment bear traps.

Throughout this book I will alert you to the key information to know and also the information you won't need to waste your time on. This unnecessary information is "white noise"; it will only distract you and waste your time without providing any substantial benefit. The investment industry is an industry of information overkill. We will focus on the essential and leave the non-essential out. Everything we do will be *priority based*: we will aim to do the best possible with your money taking into account any given set of circumstances. We will concentrate on what you absolutely must know. After all, time is money. We will deal with three important elements over and over again: facts, risk, and reward. These will shape our thinking.

The types of investments we will talk about will be investments available from a stock-broker. We will not talk about art, real estate, or collectibles except as they compare to some stock market investments. We will talk about stock market investments because I know them best. Also, these investments let you start with almost any amount of money, they have liquidity (meaning you can generally buy and sell them any business day), and they offer you a range of choices with risk levels varying from high flying to ultraconservative.

The investment world is currently undergoing many changes because of industry deregulation on July 1, 1987, so now is a good time to be exploring this environment. The big changes in the investment industry will provide some people with big opportunities.
In such times, I agree with the Chinese who do not have a symbol for "crisis": they have a two-word pictograph which means both "danger" and "opportunity". You want to be prepared to recognize the opportunity and avoid the danger.

Another one of my key beliefs is that you should make the best of your current circumstances, regardless of what they are. I will show you the most profitable means to attain your goals and how to benefit from professional investors' actions.

To sum up, the main themes of this book are
— risk and how to assess it,
— facts and how to find them,
— rewards and how to calculate them,
— making the best use of your current circumstances,
— planning for your profitable financial future.

We'll keep an open mind about any investment because the range of investment products is always expanding. You need to know what these products are and whether they may be worthwhile to you.

We'll make the best of what you have in every situation. By taking this approach, you'll find you can profit from many different circumstances. We will concentrate on choosing the right investments for the right times.

The world of investments awaits . . . .

Chapter One

GET READY

You want to be an investor. Bravo! Buying this book is the first step towards reaching your goals of building your investment portfolio and increasing your investor confidence. This isn't a think-rich-and-you'll-be-rich book. Rather, I wrote it to help you understand investments and show you how to use them to improve your financial lifestyle. Neither is this book about definitions to recite. It is about understanding concepts and applying the pertinent ones to your own personal investment circumstances in order to reach your goals.

You don't have to be Einstein to understand investment concepts and profit from them. You already know how to take information that is important and use it to your advantage. One reason many people do not invest is because they feel there is so much to know and no one to teach them what they need. Wait no longer. Here is an easy-to-understand, practical guide I have designed to help you expand your investment horizons.

WHY INVEST?
Why should you invest? You may want to accumulate wealth — to get rich. You may want to accumulate money for your retirement. You may want to protect your savings by putting them to work sensibly. Or, plainly and simple, you may want to reduce your taxes. Whatever your reasons, you want to be able to make decisions based on knowledge and experience.

I am not a person who believes investment hype, and I recommend that you don't believe it either. Let's face it, anyone who tells you that by investing only $500 you can be a millionaire is kidding himself or trying to kid you. That would be a return on investment of 2,000 times! Marketwise investors do not believe in Santa Claus or the Easter Bunny either. Making money is not a matter of wishes and magic. Investors know that you must get the facts, evaluate the risk, and take decisive action to secure a reward.

"We have no magic, we don't know any way to beat the market. We simply try to use common sense to produce the greatest possible total return. And we do it on a worldwide basis." This is how Sir John M. Templeton, founder and chairman of the Templeton group of mutual funds (which have assets of $11 billion), talks about investing in a 1987 brochure.

Investing is not always a quick process. Those who make the most money in the stock market (and subsequently keep it) are people who have invested for the long term. Good things are definitely worth waiting for, though. Think how many years it takes to obtain an education or to learn to ski or play the piano really well. Yet any such accomplishments may be of tremendous value to you today. You'll find that same type of value when you learn about investments.

WHY SOME PEOPLE DON'T INVEST

The Toronto Stock Exchange, one of the institutions for buying and selling stocks in Canada, published a major survey in December 1986 entitled *Canadian Shareowners: Their Profile and Attitudes.* Some fascinating facts emerged in this survey. One particularly interesting section presented the reasons people gave for not investing in stocks. The top three reasons were (in order): lack of money, lack of information, and fear of risk. A whopping 77% of people who did not own shares said that they didn't invest because they didn't have enough money to do so. Of those responses grouped under "lack of information," the two most common explanations were that they didn't know enough about how the stock market worked and that they lacked information about which stocks to buy. Finally, 44% of non-shareowners said that investing in stocks was too risky.

This survey confirms what I have felt for a long time: people have not been given a proper education about how to save and how to invest their money. All of this will change for you with this book. The first step is saving, which means not spending. The second step is investing, which means putting your savings to work. Later on I'll address the problems of information and of how to size up risk. But what about the first reason — not having any money or, in market talk, lack of investment funds?

If you are going to invest, you are going to need money, but where are you going to get it? *Even if you do not have any money you can start to be an investor this year.* How? Through a method I call *Painless Portfolio Building.*

When investors speak of building a portfolio, what exactly are they talking about? A *portfolio* is simply the collection of all the financial investments you own. Hardly anyone starts with a fully built portfolio. You begin it, work on it, add to it, and make adjustments to it, just as you would when building a house.

I used Painless Portfolio Building for myself when I first wanted to be an investor but was flat broke. I had to figure out a way to start my own investment portfolio with no available cash. I know this method works because I have done it. There are three Painless Portfolio Building ideas in this book. This is the first.

PAINLESS PORTFOLIO BUILDING 1

Each November — and only in November — the government of Canada sells Canada Savings Bonds (CSBs). At that time you can purchase bonds at a bank, trust company, or brokerage firm. But what if you don't have the cash to buy bonds? Luckily, some ingenious person invented the payroll deduction plan, which is now offered by many employers. (If your employer doesn't have it, you can suggest starting it. Just call the Bank of Canada for the details of how to begin the plan at your firm.)

In essence, what happens is that your employer arranges a loan to buy CSBs on behalf of all of the interested employees. Then each pay period your employer deducts from your pay cheque a certain amount of money to pay back the loan. At the end of the year the loan is totally paid back and you receive the bonds. Although you are charged interest on this loan, you also earn interest on the bonds from day one. You accomplish your savings/investing objective. It costs a bit in interest charges, but they're very minor. The key point is that it's important to get started somewhere.

By signing up for the payroll deduction plan, you are taking a giant step forward.
You are making the best of your current situation (no money) and still working towards
your goal (developing a portfolio). The strategy you are using is the payroll deduction
plan. *Strategies* are the actions you take to reach your goals. They are the bridges across
the gap between where you are now and where you want to be. By using the strategy of
participating in a payroll deduction plan, you are accomplishing some very significant
financial changes. You are starting to save on a regular basis. You are also investing your
savings in a CSB. You are conditioning your investment muscle. You are making a
declaration that you are serious about becoming an investor.

After the initial shock of the first payroll deduction, most people discover that — miracle
of miracles — it is possible to save. It's all a matter of reallocating funds. At the end of
the year, in addition to having discovered that you can manage without that bit of money
each month, you become the proud possessor of Canada Savings Bonds, the first in your
arsenal of new investments designed to take you to financial freedom. There you go. It
was painless (practically) and it started you on the road to portfolio building. Next fall,
when you sign up for a payroll deduction plan, I suggest that you cut out the
advertisement for CSBs from the newspaper and put it on your fridge to remind yourself
every day that you are progressing towards your financial goals.

I know a lot of people (including me) who buy Canada Savings Bonds by this method
every year as a good discipline for saving and accomplishing their investment objectives.
To show you how painless this is, here are the figures for the 1987/8 series of Canada
Savings Bonds (the calculations assume that you are paid every other week and therefore
will make 26 repayments):

To purchase:	*Your bi-weekly payment is:*
$100 bond	$4.01
$300 bond	$12.03
$1000 bond	$40.10

Now that's painless, don't you agree?

As I mentioned earlier, the key point to beginning a portfolio is to *get started*.
The vehicle is almost irrelevant as long as you get in the habit of doing something every
month. I do not recommend being a guinea pig with investments, trying the newest
investment of the day. I want you to develop good investment habits. This savings plan
will help you develop those good habits. Many people accumulate equity (ownership) in
their homes not because they are shrewd real estate investors but because they force
themselves to save for monthly mortgage payments. For many, it means a sacrifice, but
they realize they have to make these payments or risk foreclosure. This Painless Portfolio
Building idea amounts to the same thing: forced savings.

Some cynical people will tell you that Canada Savings Bonds are a lousy investment.
They say that the interest rate isn't very good or that there are better investments or that
it takes too long. They are missing the point. As any smart investor will tell you,
you must make the best of your situation whatever it may be. This is one of the main
themes of this book. If you don't have any money and you want to get started, this is
one good way.

Also, I have seen the faces of people in the office when the Canada Savings Bonds are distributed at the end of a payroll deduction plan. The faces of those who used the plan light up, while others look on unhappily.

Yes, there may be better investments but "better" is a relative term. The interest rate Canada Savings Bonds offer is competitive, and hundreds of thousands of people buy them each year. Also, with CSBs, you will never trap yourself because you have *liquidity*. This means you can redeem them very easily: just go to a bank, trust company, or brokerage firm and you can turn your investment into cash immediately. (With liquidity you also have flexibility to move to other investments, and this flexibility is a real asset in the financial world.)

Just because you start with a Canada Savings Bond doesn't mean that you are married to it for life. You can change your investment goals at any time, and it is nice to have a investment which you can sell any business day without any delays. Canada Savings Bonds are not just for widows, orphans, and people without investment know-how. I probably don't know one savvy investor (and I have known quite a few) who hasn't used them in their portfolio at some point.

Never let other people determine which investments are best for you. Only you can do this. Seek advice, but don't let others dictate your financial needs.

KEEPING TRACK OF YOUR MONEY
Since you now know it's possible to be an investor even if you don't have any money today, let's look at your total financial picture to assess your starting point.

Being an investor is being an entrepreneur, as far as I'm concerned. In effect, you are running your own business: the business of managing your money. Think of this business as Your Future, Unlimited. As boss of your business, you need to keep records and, above all, to control spending. And if you already have money accumulated, you want to make your money work for you, instead of leaving it in the bank or under the mattress.

Where does your money go?
One of the most enlightening things I have ever done was to keep track of how I spent *every single penny* one month. (I would never have dreamt that I spent so much on food!) This exercise is good for everyone. For one month write down *every penny you spend*. (I suggest you get an extra cheque register from your bank. It will be easy to keep this little booklet with you inside your real chequebook.) At the end of the month add up all you've spent for housing, food, clothing, transportation, entertainment, and so on. Then calculate each amount as a percentage of your monthly income. Be prepared for some real shocks. If you have ever said at the end of the month, "I wonder where all my money goes?" this exercise will give you the answer.

Put the results here (don't forget to include anything you paid for with a credit card). Work out the percentages too. (Write *in* this book. I wrote this to be a workbook which houses all of your pertinent financial data and keeps track of your progress.)

What Came In, What Went Out

Food	$_____	____%
Accommodation	$_____	____%
Household expenses	$_____	____%
Transportation	$_____	____%
Education	$_____	____%
Loans	$_____	____%
Day care	$_____	____%
Entertainment	$_____	____%
Clothing	$_____	____%
Dry cleaning, laundry	$_____	____%
Insurance	$_____	____%
Miscellaneous	$_____	____%
Total spent	$_____	100%
Total income	$_____	

Now you have an exact record of how you spent all of your monthly money. Are there some surprises in this chart? Once you have evaluated where the money goes, you are in a better position to control your spending because you know *how* you spend and *what* you spend money on. Some items, such as rent or mortgage payments, are fixed costs that you can't do anything about changing. Others, such as clothes or entertainment, are variable costs that you can control, at least to some extent.

If you thought that you couldn't afford even a $100 bond, which amounted to a $2-per-week deduction, maybe this chart will show you that you can. By spending $2 less each week, you could end up with a $100 Canada Savings Bond at the end of the year. Maybe you could walk to some destination instead of taking the transit system or your car. Maybe you could go without an ice cream cone or two. Basically we are talking about doing without some small thing each week in order to start accomplishing your financial goals. You need to build investing into your financial habits if you want to succeed.

By examining your finances this way, you gain a realistic picture of where your money goes and can better decide where you want it to go in the future. I find it interesting that the money which is left over after paying for basic necessities (fixed costs) is described as "disposable income" by some people and "discretionary income" by others. "Disposable" means "able to be disposed of," whereas "discretionary" implies more of a choice.

This exercise is for everyone. I read an article in *Chatelaine* magazine recently about people in debt. One couple had a combined income of $60,000 — and debt of $30,000.

How did this happen? Whether you are making a little money or a lot, you have the potential to end up at the end of the year in debt and without savings or investments if you don't do something about starting good financial habits today.

As the Toronto Stock Exchange survey indicates, so many people think they don't have money to invest. In many cases it is because they *choose* not to have money to invest and instead spend their money elsewhere.

MY RECOMMENDED STRATEGY: Lock up all your credit cards in a safety deposit box. (Periodically I give myself this advice, and I am always amazed at how much money I "save" when I do this.) Also, once you have the habit of keeping track of where your monthly income goes, you tend to be more careful about your spending. So keep up this practice if possible.

Keeping your records A-Z
Since you now have a base or history of how you use your money, you are clearly on your way to becoming more aware financially.

Next, go out and buy an expanding file, the kind with A–Z markings on it. Here is where you will keep your financial data, such as receipts for income tax purposes, important details of your investment transactions, and all sorts of information you will gather on saving and investing.

Although your file may seem somewhat empty now, in a few years you'll be surprised at how it overflows. Developing good record-keeping habits is absolutely crucial to your success. Develop professional investor habits because that is the type of investor you plan to be.

Sources of information
Now, go out and get a library card. Investment books and magazines are expensive, and initially you won't know which ones to purchase. If you are fortunate enough to live in a city with a large main library, spend some time there looking at all the investment publications available. Then you can decide which ones suit your style of investing. If you don't live near such a mine of information, see if your local library can order publications you're interested in. In later chapters I'll suggest some publications to consider. Remember, investing is a very personal decision, and what suits your mother may not suit you. Initially, take a look at every publication you can, just for the flavour. I suggest asking the librarians for help, as they can be invaluable sources of information.

Check your own attitudes
Finally, think seriously about your attitude toward investing. Maybe you fear that you will be taken advantage of by someone with more knowledge. The best defence is to be prepared. Maybe you grew up thinking that someone else would take care of money for you. This is unlikely in today's world, so I'd suggest you start preparing now. Maybe you think having money would somehow change your personality. Yes, you might become more confident. Maybe you've been so busy working that you haven't had a chance to get your head above water until this point, but now you're ready. Think about your own particular attitude.

Whatever your circumstances may be, it is vital to keep an open mind. You will acquire great quantities of new information from this book. Investments are constantly changing, so you must be able to roll with the punches. Who can predict the economy? Even the economists can't agree! Bennett W. Goodspeed says in his fantastic book *The Tao Jones Averages:* "Avoid depending on well-known experts. Not only have they perfected the art of going wrong with confidence, but their advice is so widely disseminated as to give no one a real advantage."

Your own opinion is valuable. I know one man who made a lot of money by guessing what would happen to the price of frozen orange juice. He thought the weather in citrus-growing country was worsening — and he was right.

You must stay flexible in order to make the best of whatever comes your way. Marketwise investing means having the ability to adapt and survive.

PROGRESSING THROUGH THIS BOOK

Although some of these first chapters may sound intimidating today, when you have completed this book with its step-by-step explanations, you will be a hundred times more confident. Take the investment world one step at a time. On your travels there, if you don't understand something you come across, make a note of it and find the answer. Seek out information.

I won't throw a million irrelevant details at you. I'll only give you what I think counts. Marketwise investing isn't a test. It's a method of doing business that will stand you in good stead for a long time.

Who knows — you could find that this book turns your interest in investments into a hobby. And as you know, many hobbies have turned into full-time occupations and businesses. Stranger things have happened.

So relax, take as much time as you need. You don't need to hurry. You control the pace, so you can feel confident when you make saving or investment decisions.

In this chapter we
  — started a Painless Portfolio Building savings program,
  — learned to keep track of where money goes,
  — started record keeping.

In the next chapter I will show you how to review your past and take inventory of your current assets so that you know your starting point. You will no longer be puzzled about where you stand financially. You'll also examine future goals so you can start developing your own individual plan.

How does it sound so far? Go ahead, admit it out loud. Even if you feel funny, go ahead and say it: *I want to control my financial future.* So let's begin.

Chapter Two

GET SET

No astute investor would advance into the future without a strategy. And neither will you! I'm going to introduce you to a few easy steps with which you can start to design your own strategy to reach your goals. The three key pieces of information you will require for this section are

- where you were five years ago,
- where you are now, and
- where you plan to be.

In other words, past, present and future. Take a few moments to concentrate and fill out the next section.

YOUR FIVE-YEAR HISTORY

Let's start with where you were five years ago. Think back on and list the achievements you have been able to make in five short years. Write down everything: career moves, education obtained, courses taken, financial improvements, personal accomplishments, family changes, new skills learned, places visited, things made and acquired. . . .
When you started many of these projects, you probably thought they would never be finished. Lo and behold, somehow they were accomplished. When you are finished doing this exercise, I am positive you will be surprised at exactly how much you have done.

Write your accomplishments of the last five years here:

_____   _____

_____   _____

_____   _____

_____   _____

_____   _____

This is your recent history. Investing is just like these achieved goals. It has a lot to do with persisting until the task is complete.

THE PRESENT

Now let's find out where you are today, looking specifically at finances. You need to know your "investor starting point" before you look at where you want to go.

The following form is based on an investment firm's financial profile for clients. You will be better prepared to meet your stockbroker or financial consultant if you take an inventory of your financial circumstances first. (Keep in mind that you don't have to fill in every space.)

It is extremely important to get this information down on paper. When reviewing details of financial plans, I found that when I actually got them down on paper, I was able to see a lot more clearly exactly where things stood in order to plan for the future. So please don't skip over these steps. They could be the difference between success and failure. If you think it takes too much time, ask yourself, "Am I worth it?". As I said before, this book is about facts, risk, and reward. Get the facts down if your goal is to be a better, more successful investor.

A Financial Snapshot of Where You Stand Today

ASSETS (WHAT YOU OWN) priced at what you could sell them for today:

— residence (house, cottage, tent) $ _____

— personal property (furniture, jewellery, art, car, baseball cards) $ _____

— cash and cash equivalents (CSBs, everything you have in the bank, what you have under your mattress) $ _____

— tax deferral vehicles (RRSPs, tax shelters, pension plans) $ _____

— securities (mutual funds, stocks, and all the other things we will discuss in the following chapters) $ _____

— other assets (only you know what these are) $ _____

TOTAL = $ _____

LIABILITIES (WHAT YOU OWE) based on today's amount owed:

— mortgage(s) $ _____

— personal loans $ _____

— money owed on your credit cards $ _____

— securities which aren't fully paid for $ _____

— other liabilities $ _____

TOTAL = $ _____

Now you subtract your liabilities from your assets. The answer is your *net worth* today. If you sold everything you own and paid off everything you owe, the amount you would have left over is your net worth. It is where you are at.

Your assets $_____ — Liabilities $_____ =

Your net worth: $_____

If the number is negative, get help. Obtain some advice before you consider investing. There are credit counselling services available. They can advise you on controlling your finances or consolidating your debts.

If the number is positive, read on.

After reviewing this snapshot, some important items may come into focus. Perhaps you see that almost everything you own is in one area; for example, all of your assets may be in your home or in deposits at a bank or trust company. This may not be the way you wish it to be in the future. But there is no denying that this is where you are today.

YOUR FUTURE

The next step is to define where you want to go. Don't worry yet about how you will get there. As they say in advertising, never confuse the how (the way you'll get to your goal) with the what (your actual goal). At this stage the important thing is to set out your goals.

I've given you a worksheet listing goals some of my clients have worked towards. Don't let this list inhibit you. If your goal is to be wealthy and living in Bora Bora by the time you reach 40, go ahead and put it down. Without dreams, how would dreams come true? Denis Waitley, in his book *Seeds of Greatness*, defines daydreams as "goals in the formative stages". So dream away.

In *Unlimited Power*, Anthony Robbins cites a recent US study showing that fewer than 10% of the population have articulated and written down their goals. *You will put yourself in an entirely different investment category simply by writing down your goals.* You both need to know and want to know where you are going.

Possible goals

In the following list, check off the goals that interest you and then rank them in your order of importance, one being the highest priority. Also, categorize them as long-term (going to take a while to get there) and short-term (maybe this year) goals.

What Do I Want for My Future?

Interested?	Priority	Long-term or short-term?	
_____	_____	_____	**develop a portfolio for retirement income and security**
_____	_____	_____	**build a fund for my children's education**
_____	_____	_____	**own my own business**
_____	_____	_____	**buy a home**
_____	_____	_____	**eliminate my mortgage and other debts**
_____	_____	_____	**attain personal/family goals (travel, pool, car, boat, furniture, renovations)**
_____	_____	_____	**make charitable donations/bequests**
_____	_____	_____	**other (go crazy and write your wildest dream here: owning a restaurant, buying diamond jewellery, travelling around the world in a sailboat, make a film. . .)** _____

_____

_____

"In planning one's life, there is always dreaming in the reality, and reality in the dreaming" (the tortoise, after he beat the hare as quoted by Richard Nelson Bolles in *What Color is Your Parachute?*)

Goals can change over the course of a lifetime. The financial goals for a young married couple who are planning to have children are dramatically different from the goals of a breadwinner who is about to retire. Gail Sheehy described this process of change in her book *Passages*. When you consider your short-term and long-term goals, you might want to think of your own financial passages. Career, education, marriage, children, travel, retirement — each of these important events in life demands a certain approach to financial planning. It's helpful to think in these terms because what was appropriate yesterday is not always appropriate tomorrow or the day after that.

MY RECOMMENDED STRATEGY: Do this goal-setting exercise each year. I do mine at New Year's, both to assess what I have done in the previous year and to set myself on the right course for the new year.

Dr. Maxwell Maltz, in his book *Psycho-Cybernetics*, compares the mind to an automatic pilot. Once it is set on its course, it adjusts all its activities to keep on track. That is why it is so important to write down your goals and to review them constantly.

Remember that goal-setting is a lifelong activity; you are never too young or too old for it. You can't change your past, but with confidence and know-how you can shape your future.

In this chapter we
— reviewed the accomplishments of the last five years of your life,
— did a financial profile of where you stand today,
— set goals for the future and prioritized them.

In the next chapter, we will examine investment routes to get you to your personal destination. Already, by knowing yourself, where you are, and what your goals are, you've made further progress towards becoming personally and financially aware.
Now you have truly useful information and a starting point for reaching your goals.

Chapter Three

GO FOR IT

Do you feel you've made progress? Since, as I said earlier, fewer than 10% of the population have written, articulated goals, you are in the upper echelon, one of those people who really want to succeed. Now I think that's progress!

One thing, I'm sure you've realized, about many of these goals is that they require money. Now we get down to the nitty gritty. Two words that constantly appear in discussions of money and investments are *safety* and *risk*. The "right stuff" in this area is knowing how to assess risk and to determine the amount of risk that is appropriate to the circumstances and to you. Since you have set your goals, we are ready to examine the concepts of safety and risk and how they relate to the strategies you want to develop.

Many people have told me that the investment world is a puzzle. The nice thing about puzzles (even the Rubik's Cube) is that they can be solved. My goal is to break down the puzzle of investments into manageable pieces for you to understand. Later in this chapter, I will introduce you to *four basic investment objectives*. You may find that only one of them is right for you. Or you may prefer a combination. Don't let the idea of multiple choices put you off. When you first hear about everything that is available with all of the fancy financial terms and concepts, you may want to throw up your hands in despair. Never fear, once you get the hang of it, you will be telling other people how simple it is.

I will show you how to take advantage of these four objectives. As I have told you from the outset, I'm going to talk about what I know best — the market — because that's where there are plenty of opportunities for investors. I want you to be one of those investors, seizing opportunities as they arise and profiting from circumstances.

SOME IMPORTANT CONCEPTS
Before we look at actual investment strategies, we need to consider a few concepts — risk, safety, the long term, and timing. And before we do that, we should focus briefly on inflation, which is one of the realities of the modern world and one of the reasons you need to put your savings to work for you.

Inflation (a costly proposition)
One item that needs addressing right away is inflation. Every month the *Consumer Price Index (CPI)* tells us how much *more* it costs us to buy things. It lets us know how prices are going up — inflating — to keep up with the rising costs of wages, taxation, transportation, and the production of goods and services. Exhibit 3.1 and 3.2 show you two different pictures of inflation. Exhibit 3.2 shows year-to-year changes in inflation and the effects on consumer prices in Canada over the last few years.

EXHIBIT 3.1
Consumer Price Index
1970 = 100

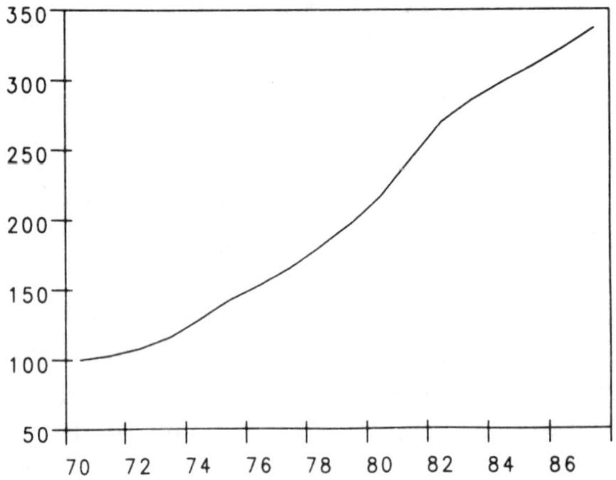

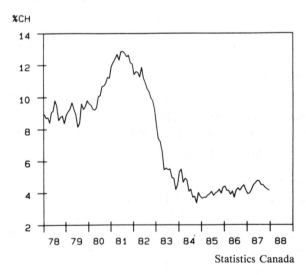

Statistics Canada

You want to compare inflation with rises in your after-tax income (what you get to take home or keep) to see if you are getting ahead or falling behind. To give you an idea of just how important this is, review Exhibits 3.3 and 3.4, which will show first the rate of return required just to stay even after you take inflation and taxation into account and then the rate of return needed to get ahead by 5%.

EXHIBIT 3.2
Inflation in Canada
(percentage change in consumer prices from year to year)

Statistics Canada

The point comes home when you think about what inflation and taxation could do to your money during the next year. In January 1988 the top five chartered banks in this country were paying interest of 4.5% on savings accounts. In early 1988 the inflation rate was about 4% and expected to stay level. And for the 1988 tax year, the government proposes to use three tax brackets as follows:

Taxable income	Income tax (federal and provincial combined)
Less than $27,000	26.0%
$27,001 - $55,000	39.8%
More than $55,000	44.4%

(Actually, differences in provincial taxation will make these rates vary across the country, but not enough to change the situation I'm describing here.)

With these tax rates, if interest rates and inflation stay as they are now, *no one who has taxable income and keeps his or her money in a savings account will break even.* To see why, look down the 4%-inflation column in Exhibit 3.3. Anyone in the first tax bracket needs more than 5.3% return to stay even, anyone in the middle bracket needs 6.7%, and anyone in the top bracket needs 7.3%.

Turn to Exhibit 3.4 to determine exactly how much you need to make in order to get ahead by 5%. You'll discover the rates are 12.3%, 15.3%, and 16.7% respectively.

Now that you understand the importance of inflation, let's move on to risk.

Risk and why I like it
I like risk. I am not talking about crazy, jump-off-a-tall-building risk, but about risk in a positive form. I believe it is absolutely crucial to understand risk in order to understand saving and investing. To me, risk is partly attitude. It means being prepared to consider any possibility. It means not eliminating any idea without looking at all the facts. It means keeping an open mind and being confident enough to say yes or no after examining the pros and cons.

My basic belief is that there are no safe investments. (I will pause here for this shocking statement to be digested.) I know this statement may upset you, but I have come to this conclusion after some very important lessons and research. Therefore I would like you to understand risk and become comfortable with it. If you do, you will have less trauma and be more in control of your life. Doesn't that sound appealing? This is not a theory I made up: it is reality to me. (When I use the terms "theory" and "reality", I am referring to what should be according to the books — theory — and what really is — reality — which is what investors want to know.)

How did I conclude that we should be comfortable with risk? I looked once again at facts, risk, and reward. The facts are that there are certain investments which are better to own under certain economic conditions. I'm thinking of short-term interest-bearing investments, such as Treasury bills when interest rates are fluctuating wildly. If things are crazy, you want to be in a liquid investment such as T-bills, which you can always sell, which are backed by the Government of Canada, and which pay you interest. You can hold this investment until things calm down, and you feel better prepared to make another investment decision. There is nothing magical about this. It is just logical.

EXHIBIT 3.3
To Maintain Your Purchasing Power,
Your Money Must Increase by . . .

Tax Rate	Inflation Rate (%)										
(%)	0	1	2	3	4	5	6	7	8	9	10
0	0	1.0%	2.0%	3.0%	4.0%	5.0%	6.0%	7.0%	8.0%	9.0%	10.0%
10	0	1.1	2.2	3.3	4.4	5.6	6.7	7.8	8.9	10.0	11.1
15	0	1.2	2.4	3.5	4.7	5.9	7.1	8.2	9.4	10.6	11.8
20	0	1.2	2.5	3.7	5.0	6.2	7.5	8.7	10.0	11.2	12.5
25	0	1.3	2.7	4.0	5.3	6.7	8.0	9.3	10.7	12.0	13.3
30	0	1.4	2.9	4.3	5.7	7.1	8.6	10.0	11.4	12.9	14.3
35	0	1.5	3.1	4.6	6.2	7.7	9.2	10.8	12.3	13.8	15.4
40	0	1.7	3.3	5.0	6.7	8.3	10.0	11.7	13.3	15.0	16.7
45	0	1.8	3.6	5.5	7.3	9.1	10.9	12.7	14.5	16.4	18.2
50	0	2.0	4.0	6.0	8.0	10.0	12.0	14.0	16.0	18.0	20.0
55	0	2.2	4.4	6.7	8.9	11.1	13.3	15.6	17.8	20.0	22.2
60	0	2.5	5.0	7.5	10.0	12.5	16.0	17.5	20.0	22.5	25.0
65	0	2.9	5.7	8.6	11.4	14.3	17.1	20.0	22.9	25.7	38.6
70	0	3.3	6.7	10.0	13.3	16.7	20.0	23.3	26.7	30.0	33.3

EXHIBIT 3.4
To Increase Your Purchasing Power by 5%,
Your Money Must Increase by . . .

Tax Rate	Inflation Rate (%)										
(%)	0	1	2	3	4	5	6	7	8	9	10
0	5.0%	6.0%	7.1%	8.1%	9.2%	10.2%	11.3%	12.3%	13.4%	14.4%	15.5%
5	5.3	6.4	7.5	8.6	9.7	10.8	11.9	13.0	14.1	15.2	16.3
10	5.6	6.7	7.9	9.1	10.2	11.4	12.6	13.7	14.9	16.1	17.2
15	5.9	7.1	8.4	9.6	10.8	12.1	13.3	14.5	15.8	17.0	18.2
20	6.2	7.6	8.9	10.2	11.5	12.8	14.1	15.4	16.7	18.1	19.4
25	6.7	8.1	9.5	10.9	12.3	13.7	15.1	16.5	17.9	19.3	20.7
30	7.1	8.6	10.1	11.6	13.1	14.6	16.1	17.6	19.1	20.6	22.1
35	7.7	9.3	10.9	12.5	14.2	15.8	17.4	19.0	20.6	22.2	23.8
40	8.3	10.1	11.8	13.6	15.3	17.1	18.8	20.6	22.3	24.1	25.8
45	9.1	11.0	12.9	14.8	16.7	18.6	20.5	22.5	24.4	26.3	28.2
50	10.0	12.1	14.2	16.3	18.4	20.5	22.6	24.7	26.8	28.9	31.0
55	11.1	13.4	15.8	18.1	20.4	22.8	25.1	27.4	29.8	32.1	34.4
60	12.5	15.1	17.7	20.4	23.0	25.6	28.2	30.9	33.5	36.1	38.7
65	14.3	17.3	20.3	23.3	26.3	29.4	32.3	35.3	38.3	41.3	44.3
70	16.7	20.2	23.7	27.2	30.7	34.2	37.7	41.2	44.7	48.2	51.7

I realize that risk comes in varying degrees. I am not living under any delusion that the stock market is composed only of reasonable investments. You just need to look at the history of various stocks in this country to know that there are some extremely high risk investments for sale out there. But, as we have seen, there is also risk in keeping your money in a savings account.

Don't kid yourself that every investment is great, wonderful, and only mildly risky. This is not the case. For all investments you need to assess the risk and the reward by looking at the best-case scenario and the worst-case scenario for what could happen to your money, given the information you know today.

Safety: What's that?
Safe and safety are such unusual terms. There are safety matches (they work for a pyromaniac), a safety razor (which still has the potential to cut you), and a safecracker (who will take away the decision you have to make about your valuables — by taking them from you).

When I lecture on investments, one of my favourite questions is "What is a safe investment?". It gets everyone thinking! Assuming (in general) that "safe" means holding its value or providing a rate of return above and beyond inflation and taxation, the answers to this question almost always fall into one of four categories: (1) real estate, (2) gold, (3) interest-bearing certificates (term deposits, Canada Savings Bonds, bank accounts), and (4) the stock market.

Hindsight is always 20-20, but I think that examining some basic historical facts about each of these answers will provide you with some valuable insight. Remember, these investments are commonly believed to be safe.

Real estate
If you had purchased residential real estate in Toronto as an investment in the first week of April 1981, you would have had to wait until 1984 for it to return to what you paid for it.

Mind you, if you had purchased real estate in 1984, you would have doubled your money in two years.

What was the difference? The economic circumstances which prevailed in 1981 differed from those of 1984. In early 1981 the inflation rate was 12% and the interest rate was 15%. In late 1981 the interest rate was 20%, preventing almost everyone from investing in real estate. In order to invest in the real estate market, you would have had to believe that you could make more than your carrying costs per year (mortgage, taxes, heating, hydro, water, maintenance, and so on) plus your opportunity cost (the return you would have made by investing the money elsewhere, such as in a term deposit or Canada Savings Bonds).

In late 1984 you had interest rates at a relatively more acceptable level of 13% and falling, which caused more people to consider the real estate market as an appropriate investment.

Is real estate a safe investment? Yes, at certain times, and no, at other times. The economic facts often determine whether an investment is the right investment for the time.

This example highlights a typical investment circumstance. You will find that many things in the investment world work on a seesaw basis. If something goes up, something else goes down. Interest rates were high, so housing prices declined since people couldn't afford to buy a home and carry a mortgage. When interest rates declined, the real estate market improved because people could once again afford to buy a house and pay the carrying charges.

Gold

Because gold is hard currency and tangible, it is often cited as a safe investment. You may remember a picture on the front page of many newspapers in 1982. Out the door and down the street went a lineup of people who wanted to purchase gold from a bank. That was the top of the gold market — the price was more than $700 US an ounce — and gold hasn't seen that high price again. Over the next two years it dropped to a low of $290 US, before it rose again.

This, of course, is only recent history. If you had been a real hotshot, you would have purchased gold when it was $35 (US) an ounce (before 1975) and not really cared too much when it dropped to $290 since that amount still gave you a substantial return on your investment.

Why did gold rise to such heights and then drop? Remember that oil prices were extremely high in 1982 and problems in the Middle East were rampant. People were trying to find something "international" that would keep its value. Of course, many other things also contributed to this fluctuation, but it suffices to say that events and economic circumstances caused gold to move in price.

The next time someone tells you gold is the only safe investment, smile and say yes it is, under certain economic, political, or social circumstances. As a marketwise investor you will come to know proclamations are not gospel. The key is to examine the circumstances at the time and make a decision that suits you.

Interest-bearing certificates

Any investment that gives you interest income falls into the category of an interest-bearing certificate. The most attractive example in recent history was Canada Savings Bonds in November 1981 offering 19.5%. Glory hallelujah! But despite this high rate, some people actually made a *negative* rate of return on them.

To see why, think about those two facts of life: inflation and taxation. Financially speaking, these are two of the worst things that can happen to you. Inflation eats away at what your money can buy for you. Taxation eats away at what you get to take home from your earnings or income.

Now let's reconsider that 19.5% interest on Canada Savings Bonds. People who bought them knew that the risk was extremely low, since the bonds are backed by the Government of Canada (also known as us, the people). At first glance, the rate of return of

19.5% seems like a great reward for a low-risk investment. *But* the average rate of inflation from November 1981 to October 1982, the time period for the 19.5% interest rate, was more than 11%. For anyone in the top tax bracket, the 1982 tax rates were about 50%. With these figures in hand we can determine the value of this investment.

Interest rate 19.5% − taxation of 50% = 9.75%
After-tax rate of return 9.75% − inflation rate of 11% = −1.25%.

That's a negative rate of return of 1.25%. Does this shock you? Althought there are all sorts of little refinements on your tax form that are supposed to ensure that inflation doesn't eat away all of your money, the facts of the matter are that for those people in this economic circumstance with this investment, things did not look good. This outcome does not fit the standard criteria of "safe", meaning holding its value or providing a rate of return.

If an investor in another tax bracket bought CSBs in 1981, however, he or she would have made a positive rate of return. This is why all economic factors and your personal circumstances must be considered before classifying anything as safe or risky.

What would have happened if, in March 1982, you had purchased a term deposit offering 16% for five years for your registered retirement savings plan? Gains in RRSPs, remember, are not taxed (more on this in Chapter Ten), so you would have reaped great rewards. Over the next five years people got rates between 9 and 13% for five-year term deposits. Congratulations to my father for doing this without even consulting me. Once again, your goal is to assess the risk and attempt to profit from the specific circumstances.

The stock market
The *Toronto Stock Exchange 300 Composite index* is an indicator of how the stock market as a whole is performing. This index is composed of 300 stocks trading on the Toronto Stock Exchange (TSE) and tells you each business day whether the market has risen or fallen over the previous day.

It works like this. In 1975 someone at the TSE added up the values of all 300 companies in this index (the values totalled $36 billion) and used this number to set the TSE Composite index value at 1000. The values of those 300 companies were added up again the next day and the day after that and so on right up to the present. The various securities are weighted in the index, so their average prices and the index don't rise or fall in exact correspondence, but you get the general idea.

If media announcers tell you, "The TSE 300 was up by two points," this means that the total values of the 300 companies in the index has increased by $1.82 million from the previous day's total. Of course, individual stocks among those 300 rarely follow the average exactly. If the index has risen, probably some stock prices have risen, some have fallen, and some have stayed the same price. The index is simply a general barometer of the direction of the stock market.

To give you another perspective, to have a 1% change in the total value of the companies in the index, the TSE 300 index would have to move by 33 points. Exhibit 3.5 is a graph of the movements of the TSE 300 index over recent years. Here is a chart of the index to show you its movements. Remember, a rising index means rising stock prices.

EXHIBIT 3.5

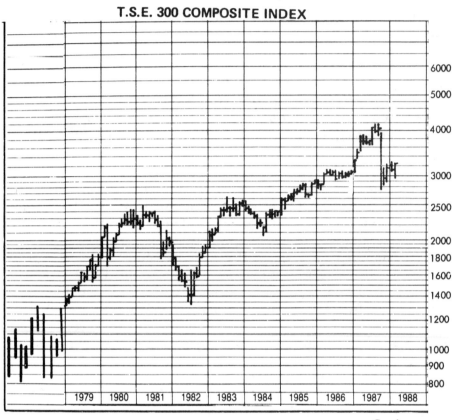

T.S.E. 300 COMPOSITE INDEX

Graphoscope

If you had entered the stock market in January 1976 and your choices followed the pattern of the TSE 300 index, virtually nothing would have happened to your investment until April 1978, almost two and one-quarter years later. (One killer in the stock market is boredom.) But if you had invested in April 1978, you could have doubled your money in the next two years.

In August 1981 we saw the market fall out of bed, as they say. The TSE 300 index dropped from 2400 to 1350 by August 1982 — a 44% decline over one year. Talk about negative rate of return! But you might have invested in the stock market then. The question is always "Is this danger or opportunity?" If you had decided it was opportunity and put your money into the stock market in August 1982, you would have seen the index triple in five years, moving to almost 4000 by April 1987. (Remember that not every stock would have tripled in value. But on the whole, there was a dramatic rise in prices.)

To get a long-term perspective, let's go back and assess the time period from April 1976 to April 1987. The index was at 1100 in April 1976 and 4000 in April 1987. That is a rate of return of 264% over 11 years or 24% each year in raw terms (264% ÷ 11 = 24%), despite the dipsy doodling of the market. So if you had just bought stock and held on, weathering the boredom, the storm, and the good times, you would have done really well.

Wait a minute, you say. You didn't put inflation or taxation into your calculation. Well, from April 1976 to April 1987 inflation virtually doubled the Consumer Price Index. Factor in inflation, and you would still have had a before-tax rate of return of about 12% (24% ÷ 2) on that 1976–1987 investment. The effect of taxation is more difficult to calculate. Since tax regulations change frequently and your tax bracket may have changed, it is difficult to compute an after-tax rate of return here. But I'm sure you'd agree that you would have made money, the purpose of the exercise.

Economists would argue that these figures are not exact, but I think they illustrate the point I am making and let you see the concept at work. True investors realize that investing for the long run is vital. A raw 24% rate of return provides, after inflation, a 12% before-tax rate of return. You need to apply your appropriate tax rate to find your *real* rate of return, the rate you receive after inflation and taxation.

Long-term investing and why it pays
The people who invest for the long run are the ones who do the best with the least amount of trauma and hysteria. I know I keep returning to this point, but it's vital. A really long-term study was done by two professors at the University of Western Ontario's Business School and published in 1988. Professors James Hatch and Robert White, in *Stocks, Bonds, Bills and Inflation*, compared the after inflation performance of common stocks with that of "safe" investment vehicles such as bonds and Treasury bills. They concluded that over the long term — December 31, 1949 to December 31, 1987 — the rates of return on the stock market were indisputably the best. They gave the results of $1 invested in December 1949. Invested in long-term bonds, $1 would have been worth $1.27 in 1987; invested in T-bills it would have been worth $1.55; and invested in common stocks it would have been worth $9.47. As you can see, these figures show that owning stocks provided a rate of return at least six times greater than the traditional safe vehicles.

I do not think that "safe" can be used to categorize investments ahead of time. Only in hindsight can you calculate returns and determine which investments have proved safest. That is why I continue to stress that facts, risk, and reward are the key tools for an investor. With these you can determine the right investment for the right time, the investment that will take you towards your goals.

Timing
The key factor in all these examples, the one which made the difference between profit and no profit, was *timing*. It was the result of looking at the facts, assessing the risk, and evaluating the potential reward before deciding which action to take. It is you who must determine that the time is right for you. Everyone talks about timing, but not very many people can do it precisely. It is a difficult task so I feel that getting *close* to the right time is really what you should be aiming for. There's no point in trying to fool yourself into thinking that you can become a genius at market timing. People have tried to do that for years. What you can do is to apply your common sense to a given economic situation, try to be close in your timing, and invest for the long term. As Philip Fisher says in *Common Stocks and Uncommon Profits*, "It's a good deal easier to know *what's* going to happen than *when* it's going to happen."

Risk, safety, long-term investing, and timing are all points you'll want to consider and determine for yourself.

STRATEGIES

Enough for now of the large-scale, historical picture. Let's look at where you are today in your investing lifetime. If you are willing to go along with me and my convictions about safety and risk, followed me as I turn to the actions you can take to achieve your goals.

As I said earlier, you can do two things with your money, if you don't want to spend it all. You can accumulate (save) it, or you can invest it. Your investment strategies will involve variations on these two actions.

Every strategy has an objective. The following list of four basic objectives can help you clarify what you're going to do with your money to reach your goals.

Basic investment objectives

Which objective suits you at this moment? Regardless of whether or not you are an investor now, you can select an investment approach that you think would fit your investment needs. Most investments fall into the following broad categories: regular income, low-risk growth, high-risk growth, and tax savings. Don't be surprised if your needs require you to be in more than one category.

Regular income

This objective is met by any investment that pays you on a regular basis without requiring you to sell the security. This means that you get a cheque basically for being an owner of the security. The income you receive comes in the form of interest or dividends.

Typical forms: Savings accounts, term deposits, Canada Savings Bonds, other bonds, debentures, preferred shares, some common shares, and interest-income mutual funds.

Don't worry if you don't yet know what all of these different investments are, I will explain them very shortly. The basic idea here is to determine whether you want to have regular income from your investments or whether you choose investments which didn't pay you now. Many very good investments don't pay off now because the company you've invested in is still using all its money to continue growing. Potentially, it could grow at an even greater rate than the income you would have received if you had chosen a term deposit. The assumption is that if you opt for a longer-term investment, the growth potential compensates you for giving up current income.

Another very important fact to keep in mind is that if you are receiving a hefty income, such as interest, from an investment, the chances of also making a hefty profit from later selling the same investment are slim. Here is the perennial risk-and-reward seesaw.
The rule of thumb is the greater the potential reward, the greater the risk for your money. There is no free lunch and no perfect investment. Therefore, look at all angles, meaning those best- and worst-case scenarios.

Low-risk growth

Any investment which outperforms taxation and inflation without making you bite your nails up to your elbow can fall into this category. With this objective, you invest in instruments for the potential growth that could result from smart management and good products on the part of the company and the right economic circumstances. (You see, even companies need to interpret economic circumstances carefully in order to be successful.)

Typical forms: stock market investments such as shares of common stocks, convertible preferred shares, convertible bonds or debentures, and many mutual funds.

These investments may provide you with some income, but not as much as the securities chosen by investors seeking regular income. What you really want here is a chance to make money from the long-term growth potential of certain securities, but you don't want to go crazy waiting for it to happen.

High-risk growth
Into this category falls any investment which offers you greater-than-average rewards — accompanied, of course, by greater risk. You should make such an investment with full knowledge of its potential for greater loss than with low-risk or regular-income investments.

Typical forms: everything from warrants, rights, growth stocks, and stock in junior companies, right up to options, commodity futures, and penny stocks (also known as penny dreadfuls — for good reasons).

Again you have a descriptive term "high-risk growth" which means something different to everyone. For people who have never been in the market before, shares of Bell Canada Enterprises, one of the lowest-risk stocks available, may seem like a high-risk investment. Others feel it's okay to roll the dice for big stakes. Some of the rollercoaster investments may be the only ones that can provide the excitement of big potential gains and the threat of equally awesome losses, which some people want.

Tax savings through tax products (alias special investment products or, as known to most people, tax shelters)
By their very nature, these investments specifically offer the potential for certain tax benefits. They can be as mild mannered as a registered retirement savings plan or as exotic as a movie unit (designed to stimulate investment in the Canadian film industry) or a real estate partnership.

These types of investments are designed so that everyone benefits. They encourage investors to provide money to stimulate growth in certain areas, therefore, the government does not have to supply that money and in exchange is willing to allow companies to take their tax write-offs and transfer them to the investor. In other words, the companies get needed capital (money) in exchange for foregoing some of their future tax benefits.

Typical forms: registered retirement savings plans (RRSPs), real estate investments such as partnerships, and natural resource partnerships.

People using these products should be in a taxable position that justifies their buying something that helps them invest for rewards in the future while reducing their taxes today.

Knowing about these four categories is important in itself and because it can start you thinking about asset mix. Remember, in Chapter Two I said that you might find that your assets have been primarily in one area and that that may not be how you want things to be in the future. *Asset mix* is the percentage of your financial assets that you want to have in each of three areas:

- cash (or its equivalent, such as chequing or savings accounts, Treasury bills, and other very liquid investments),
- bonds,
- stocks.

Your strategy is an important factor to consider in determining exactly how much you eventually intend to have in each category.

Combining the four categories

Now that we have looked at the basic categories of investment, the fun begins.
Let's assemble the four objectives into one picture — one to help you describe your investment needs. Using the lines below, assign one to ten points to each of the investment categories according to your needs and preferences. The total should add up to ten. For example, you could give two points to tax products, five points to regular income, and three points to low-risk growth. Or you can give all ten points to one category.

Regular income	_____	points
Low-risk growth	_____	points
High-risk growth	_____	points
Tax savings	_____	points
Total investment	10	points

Warning: This calculation is not perfect (neither is the investment world). Some investments fall under more than one category. For example, Journey's End, a company which handles low-cost motel accommodation, has created a real estate partnership whose units fall under three of the four categories. This instrument provides tax benefits, provides income, and has the potential, in my opinion, for low-risk growth.

Despite the uncomfortableness you may feel initially, it is useful to start thinking in these terms. You'll find it valuable to identify your objectives at this time so that you can select vehicles that will help you to carry out your strategies of accumulating and investing. Complete the exercise because it's important to your money management. The chart will give you a focus and something which you can compare to your current investments. When you have finished this book, you will want to reassess your position. You may then want to change strategies. On the other hand, you may confidently confirm your present opinion.

MY RECOMMENDED STRATEGY:

You should do this exercise at least once a year. Over time your objectives or strategies or desired asset mix may change as your needs change or the economy alters course. Remember that flexibility is one of the keys to successful investing. I do not mean flightiness or taking the latest rage but willingness to change in response to new information. When economic, political, social, or personal circumstances change, you want to be able to move with the current.

As Bernard Baruch says in his book, *Baruch, My Own Story:*

> One cannot, in other words, make an investment and take for granted that its
> worth will remain unchanged. New sources of supply coming from hitherto
> untapped areas of the world may transform the competitive position of a
> company, as will changes in people's habits or technological innovations. Often
> something will shrink in value because of one discovery, as coal did in relation
> to oil and electricity, only to be given new economic life by another develop-
> ment such as the new chemical uses being made of coal.

Although I have concentrated on economic circumstances, keep in mind that political and
social circumstances are equally capable of moving the stock market. For instance, in 1981
when the government brought in the National Energy Program, designed to increase
national ownership in oil companies in Canada, all oil stocks declined as investors realized
their potential for profit had been reduced. When Inco, a mining company, was cited as
causing severe pollution, this social and environmental issue depressed the stock's price.
Many people did not wish to support what the company was doing and sold their shares;
others feared that increased government regulation of pollution would reduce the firm's
profits.

INVESTMENT ATTITUDES

Moving now to personalities. I am going to give you broad definitions of certain types of
investors. This is not a financial horoscope, but you may find your personality reflected
here.

Please note that the four objectives we just reviewed and the four investment personalities
described here do not necessarily coincide. To have an objective of regular income does
not necessarily coincide with being an ultra-conservative risk-taker. Each objective can be
met with high-risk and low-risk investments, and under the types of investors are high-risk
and low-risk tolerances for various securities. Use the following information to round out
your ideas and determine more clearly your own comfort level with various investment
actions.

Ultra-conservative risk-taker

Certainty is your watchword. Income is your desired outcome. The key question for you
is what is the source of income and how secure do both the income and the investment
appear to be.

Be honest with yourself: would you stay awake at night worrying about your investments?
The answer is important. Some people find investing their money so troublesome that they
really do toss and turn all night. If this is you, then be ultra-conservative: keep your
money in the bank, Treasury bills, Canada Savings Bonds, or a combination of these
financial instruments. These savings vehicles and investments under the regular income
category would suit you best, regardless of other people's advice about better investments.

The only thing you might begin to ask yourself is whether you would take a different
course of action with your investments if you knew more about the alternatives and the
risk involved. In other words is it lack of knowledge and lack of confidence that is
keeping you in this category?

For you, reading this book may be your first step towards exploring alternatives.
You need to understand what is really happening to your money before you consider the alternatives available. Don't try anything new yet. Remember, the smart investor is the one who can comprehend the risk and decide the level that is personally acceptable. You may have already determined that a risk level close to zero is for you. On the other hand, you may be willing to look at alternatives after having studied them in depth.

Moderate risk-taker

You are prepared to invest and wait for a return on your money that is potentially better than what's available to the ultra-conservative investor. Income may not be critical to you.

It is important to determine for yourself the length of time that you are willing to wait for your investment to pay off — is it six months or six years? It is also important to determine the amount of growth that you are seeking. One basic definition is that the investment must outperform taxation and inflation, but you must determine if that is your definition of growth.

This book offers advice about types of moderate-risk investments that could fall under any of the four investment objectives. Review all of them in order to keep your own strategy in top form.

High risk-taker

You crave high risk, and you are always striving for growth. You are sometimes labelled a speculator or a gambler — and you may be, but you may be just a shrewd and timely investor. Certainly, you are prepared to risk greater potential loss in order to achieve greater potential rewards. Very few people like to lose money, but in order to make really big money there is obviously going to be big risk. Otherwise, everyone would be doing it, and none of us would be working for a living. Also, remember that risk is a personal thing and that one person's high risk may be another's casual investment.

High-risk investors are able to find investments in all four categories. Since super growth is the desired goal, the vehicle hardly matters. Whatever gets you there will do.

I'll warn you that I've seen many so-called high risk-takers become despondent over losing money. Understand the risk and face the facts squarely to know that you could lose big. Recently a woman from an investment club called me for advice about its portfolio. The members had put some money into a high-risk investment, ''just for fun'', and they added more money until finally one-half of their money was invested in this one ''fun'' stock. Then the stock stopped trading (I'll explain this situation later — basically they couldn't buy or sell it), and they faced the stark realization that they could lose the entire amount they had invested. I wondered how much ''fun'' her group was having then. Don't let things get out of hand, and don't pretend you are a high roller when you aren't. It can be a very expensive pretense.

Tax-driven investor

Your prime motivation is to shelter your income from taxation. Many such investors are in the high tax brackets and therefore subject to more taxation and more of a desire to reduce it than other people. But just about all of us believe we pay too much in taxes.

Investments can provide opportunities not just for the big guys but for everybody to save some money in one way or another. Of course, the tax savings must be balanced by the fact that there is risk associated with making investments.

What kind of investor are you?
Using the previous descriptions, fill in the type of investor you feel you are:

_____

When I completed this exercise, I found I am a combination of tax-driven investor and moderate risk-taker, whereas I have a friend who is a high risk-taker.

Now combine this with your investment objectives (regular income, low-risk or high-risk growth, tax savings):

Objectives _____

COMBINING GOALS AND STRATEGIES
Pulling together what we've done so far, let's consider a goal of buying a house. One way of thinking about it is shown in Exhibit 3.6. You want a house, and you are standing in the middle of an almost infinite range of choices. Let's assume you don't have any money now to put towards your goal. Then your immediate strategy must be to save money earmarked for the eventual purchase of a house. Your choice is how to save it: buy a Canada Savings Bond through a payroll deduction plan? stop smoking and bank the price of a carton of cigarettes every week? take all your loose change every night and stuff it into a sock?

EXHIBIT 3.6
Reaching an Ultimate Goal

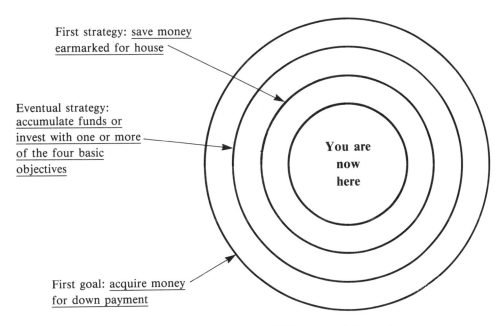

First strategy: save money earmarked for house

Eventual strategy: accumulate funds or invest with one or more of the four basic objectives

You are now here

First goal: acquire money for down payment

Ultimate goal: buy a house

After a while you have a little money, but not enough to meet that first goal of making a down payment. But now your choices of strategy are broader. You can continue just to save. And/or you can invest some of your funds, selecting your instrument for regular income, low-risk growth, or high-risk growth. (Tax savings — usually the fourth possible objective — isn't applicable in this example, but it would have been a few years ago when Revenue Canada permitted a tax deduction for participating in a Registered Home Ownership Savings Plan.) You make your choice based on your circumstances and your attitude towards risk.

Eventually you will meet the first goal and be ready to move on to the broader one of buying the house and carrying a mortgage.

As Adam Smith says in his fantastic book, *The Money Game*, "If you don't know who you are, the stock market is an expensive place to find out." Keep in mind that the more you know, the more confidence you will have about yourself, your goals, and your risk tolerance. This will stand you in good stead once you are face to face with a stockbroker. Now that you are equipped with this self-knowledge, you are ready to meet the person who can help you accomplish your financial goals: the stockbroker.

As you can see, the whole is a step-by-step procedure. Later in this book, we'll return to this picture, and you'll work out how to meet one of your goals.

In this chapter we have explored
- the effects of inflation and taxation,
- understanding safety and risk,
- four key investment objectives: regular income, low-risk growth, high-risk growth, and tax benefits,
- asset mix,
- four broad types of investor: the ultra-conservative risk-taker, the moderate risk-taker, the high risk-taker, and the tax-driven investor.

Chapter Four

YOU AND YOUR STOCKBROKER

The world of investments is one which intrigues many people and yet one which very few people know a great deal about. At parties people ask me questions about the market and about certain investments, and it seems to me that they are crying out for help.
I sympathize with the position these people are in, but a casual conversation in a party environment is not the best place to help them. What to do?

The majority of people want to have someone *to advise* them on their financial affairs. While some people can do all of the financial planning, research work, and evaluation of different investments themselves, most need assistance. Most investors *want* to have someone who can advise them, teach them, and watch out for events and information which could affect their finances and investments. That person could be a stockbroker.

WHY HAVE A STOCKBROKER?
Some people feel they don't need anyone to advise them. They believe that they know enough already. But let's go back to the idea of facts, risk, and reward. Fact: the world of finance changes daily. Risk: this influx of new information presents a large problem to someone who is trying to keep informed. Reward: obtaining an advisor to help identify these changes and how they affect particular circumstances so that the individual can make profitable decisions, when required, can save investors a lot of money.

MY RECOMMENDED STRATEGY: If you are going to venture into the world of investments, I suggest that you find an advisor, a professional whose job it is to stay informed.

You also want to have a stockbroker for time management reasons. If you are like most people and work a full week, you probably do not have the time to be as up-to-date and knowledgeable about what is happening in the marketplace as someone whose full-time job is to follow the market.

Other factors also help determine whether you need a stockbroker. These other criteria include whether you like to keep your securities in your own possession or not, how you pay for your investments, and what type of orders you place. (We'll talk about all of these items in this book.) But in general I can say that if you can do all of your own research and use only your own advice, in all likelihood you do not need a stockbroker. You would be better to go to a discount broker, who gives no advice but does offer lower commissions. If, on the other hand, you want professional advice from someone who follows the market full time, the person you want is a stockbroker.

WHO IS A STOCKBROKER?
People who make their living by advising on financial matters and charging a commission (fee) for the work they do have various titles. Broker, registered representative, financial consultant, account executive, and investment executive are all terms I have heard to describe the person known to most of the population as a stockbroker.

It may surprise you that many brokers had fascinating careers before they came into the brokerage business. Accountants, business owners, insurance people, sales people, and even investors have all joined brokerage firms. I know one person who became a successful stockbroker when she lost money in the stock market and was determined to find out why. Having had previous careers means that stockbrokers bring a wealth of knowledge and experience to their new career. Never assume that the length of time a person has been a stockbroker is the only indicator of his or her experience.

HOW DO YOU FIND A STOCKBROKER?
Time and time again people ask me the same question: do you know a good broker? My response is always yes. Every single solitary stockbroker out there is a good broker, for someone. Now, the important question is who would be a good stockbroker for you?

You must examine the following four points before you can figure out who would be good for you. Doing some soul-searching before reaching for the phone to find a stock-broker is time well spent. Answer the following questions honestly:

- How much attention do you need? Do you want the broker to spend a lot of time with you? How often do you expect to be called and updated?

- How much are you going to invest now? How much in the future? Do you know where you currently stand financially?

- What kind of investments are you interested in? How much do you know about these investments? How much would you need to be taught?

- What kind of investment temperament do you have? Do you always need to be in control or are you willing to take advice? Do you find making decisions an easy process?

The answers to these questions are guidelines for locating the type of person with whom you want to deal.

You can start by asking for a referral from friends and associates who are known to you as investors. If you don't know anyone, select brokerage firm names that sound familiar from the *Yellow Pages* (they are listed there as Stock and Bond brokers). Most brokerage firms have many branch offices in different cities. Every province in Canada has several firms represented there.

When you first call a brokerage firm, ask for the sales manager. Tell the manager a bit about your situation. Review your goals and investment strategy preferences from Chapters Two and Three, so that you can tell the sales manager about yourself.

For example, after introducing yourself you might say, "I'm not comfortable with high risk, yet I am not looking for income. I have $3000 to invest at this time. I am new to the market and therefore need someone who can explain things to me. Please refer me to someone you think I could work with."

Use your own words to convey the essential points: how much you have to invest, your general objectives and attitude towards risk (very briefly), and the specialities that interest you (if any, but you don't need this). Don't be afraid to ask questions, and above all don't be afraid to say how much you have available for investment.

Keep in mind that there are hundreds of different stocks and hundreds of different stockbrokers. You don't have to hire the first one you see. Some brokers are the first-hand kind. One colleague of mine goes to Val d'Or, Quebec to check up personally on some of the mining properties that companies own. Another associate carefully follows who's who at the companies, in order to examine their thinking and calculate how this will affect corporate results. Some specialize in high-risk ventures while others work strictly on income securities. You need to find the one who will specialize in you and your objectives.

If you are starting small ($500 to $2000), be sure that you ask whether the firm's brokers have time available to handle an account of that size. If they don't, ask them to refer you to a firm which will handle your account. There is someone out there for you.

Why a new stockbroker might be just perfect for you
If you don't have lots of money to invest or if you are a new investor, don't be dismayed if you are advised to speak with a broker who is relatively new to the industry. There are distinct benefits to dealing with eager, new individuals. These people are up-to-date because they have recently completed their firms' training programs. What they may lack is experience, something which the more established brokers have, but they don't lack investment education.

Your account may be given priority by a broker who is just beginning and has more time to spend with you. More established brokers have many accounts to take care of. This is one good reason why the best stockbroker for you may not be the number one broker in the firm. Also, you are growing in your knowledge and experience, and there may be an advantage in learning with a newer broker. There are pros and cons to every relationship, so determine your needs and look for a broker who meets them.

MEETING WITH YOUR PROSPECTIVE STOCKBROKER
Now you have received the name of a prospective broker. You have set up a meeting. It's probably scheduled for early or late in the day or at lunchtime. (Market hours are 9:30 a.m. to 4:00 p.m. Eastern Standard Time. Stockbrokers tend to schedule meetings outside those hours.) Keep in mind two main points:
* it's your money, and
* you're not afraid to ask questions so that you clearly understand what's happening.

To get ready for the meeting, you have prepared your financial information and goals based on Chapters Two and Three. Be sure to have in hand the complete details (terms, dates, and other relevant information) of your current investments whether they be registered retirement savings plans, Canada Savings Bonds, guaranteed investment certificates, or other securities.

You should also arrive at the meeting comfortable with your preferred style of investment. As you recall from Chapter Three, the style of investment indicates your attitude towards risk and growth and what level of risk is acceptable to you.

My boss tells me that when he is asked what determines a good financial consultant, he replies that the person must ask lots of questions in order to understand the client's finances inside and out *before* making any recommendations. Any stockbroker who isn't doing this is advising you with only limited information at his or her disposal.

One of my big complaints about the way stockbrokers used to do business was that they worked backwards. They would telephone you with an idea for investment, tell you what it could do for you, and then maybe they would ask you what your goals were. I feel that first you need to determine where you want to go (goal-setting), then decide on a way to get there (the strategy), and finally pick the securities (the specifics) that will assist you in reaching your goal. In the old days brokers simply sold stocks and bonds. New products and new times require new attitudes and understanding.

Stockbrokers must follow the know-your-client rule
At the outset of the meeting, state clearly (if the prospective broker doesn't beat you to it) that you understand that the information the two of you will discuss is confidential.

The number one rule for any broker — a requirement of the Canadian Securities Commission (CSC), the body that licenses all stockbrokers — is know your client.
The broker will ask you questions about your finances, what you own, your experience as an investor, and your anticipations for the future. It is an industry regulation that these questions be asked, and it is in your best interest to answer them fully. Your broker needs this information, and it is critically important that you feel comfortable sharing this confidential data. One reason for this interview is to find out if you and the prospective broker are on the same wave length.

How do you know whether the person you are speaking to is the right broker for you? Ask yourself whether this person is listening to you? You should be speaking more than the broker at this meeting. Does he or she understand your goals and your point of view? You are trying to determine whether this person gives you a feeling of confidence. Do you think that he or she can help you to carry out your objectives? You do not have to make a commitment at the first meeting. Try asking a prospective broker about the best and the worst advice he or she ever gave — and why.

Do not even take your chequebook when you sit down with a prospective broker; then you won't need to worry about whether you are going to have to buy something. You want to feel confident that this person has your best interests at heart and can help you to attain your goals.

Remember that an interview is two-way communication, not an inquisition on either side. You are there to determine if you can establish a working relationship with this stockbroker, and he or she is determining the same thing about you.

What to expect from the interview
At the end of the meeting you can expect:
- some research material,
- some suggestions to consider,
- a promise of a phone call once the stockbroker has had a chance to evaluate the information and goals you have set down,
- written material prepared by the broker, which will come in the mail later, or
- the request that you prepare some more material before specific suggestions are made.

At my firm, the financial consultants are required to do a financial profile (somewhat similar to the one you have already completed) before making recommendations. It just makes sense to look at the big picture before suggesting specific actions.

Keep reminding yourself — when in doubt — that this is your money. If you do not feel compatible with the prospective broker, call the sales manager and ask to meet another person or call another firm. All you need to say is that you would like to speak with another broker. You don't need to explain. You must feel comfortable with and have confidence in the person with whom you will be working.

As Gerald M. Loeb states in his classic, must-read volume, *The Battle for Investment Survival*, in discussing the good investment advisor:

> It is obvious that absolute 100% scrupulous honesty, combined with a real code of ethics, is the first requirement. I have already said it required genius. It takes a flexible mind. . . . It takes someone who really appreciates the risks, as over-confidence is usually fatal.

In general, I recommend that you avoid firms which only want to sell you stocks. A broker who is a stock picker (who does no planning and just picks stocks) will never be able to formulate a financial plan for you. He or she may be great for choosing certain stocks, and eventually you may even want to use someone for that specific purpose. But the purpose of financial planning is to look at the entire picture.

This brings up the point of having more than one stockbroker. Many people see it as a sign of importance to have more than one person chasing after their business. Obviously, there are pros and cons. Having information coming to you from a number of sources may help you to make better decisions. On the other hand, if you have complete trust and confidence in one person, you are more likely to share all of your financial information with that individual and to know that he or she is looking after your best interests. You need to decide what works best for you as the client.

YOUR INVESTMENT PROTECTION PLAN
All stockbrokers must follow the rules listed in the *Manual for Registered Representatives*, our book of regulations. I already mentioned the know-your-client rule, which comes from this organization. The Canadian Securities Commission is part of your consumer protection plan. Non-compliance with its rules means warnings, fines, jail sentences, or eviction from the industry for the stockbroker.

Just as there are generally acceptable accounting practices, there are generally acceptable brokerage practices. If, for example, you are a 65-year-old who is retired, you should not receive high-risk investment suggestions, and a broker could jeopardize his or her entire career by making them to you. Therefore, if you want something outside the norm for someone of your age or experience, you must specifically state that to your broker, and don't be surprised if you're asked to put it in writing for the file. This doesn't mean that you can't go outside the norms (after all, it's your money). Just as a doctor may tell you that skydiving is bad for your heart at age 70, if you still want to do it, nothing and nobody will stop you. You simply may have to confirm in writing that you are ready and able to assume the risk.

WHY CLIENT/BROKER RELATIONSHIPS STOP WORKING

Things may start off on a wonderful note with your stockbroker, but suddenly you are no longer satisfied. Why do relationships between brokers and clients break down? I'm sure you've heard people say, "My broker doesn't do this" or "My broker never did that". What happened? Many times it is simply a breakdown in communication.

When discussing communications, I am always reminded of comedian David Steinberg's rendition of a psychiatrist meeting with a patient. *Doctor:* So, what seems to be the problem? *Patient:* Doctor, I have trouble communicating. *Doctor:* I don't understand.

You must tell your broker what you expect. If the broker can't help you, you must know that, too. He or she must also tell you what can be done. The key is to keep the lines of communication open, which means that each party has to verbalize his or her wishes.

Sometimes a breakdown of verbalization is the broker's fault and sometimes it is the client's fault. Regardless of whose fault it is, when communication stops happening, trouble begins. Keep talking. It's your money at stake. If you don't like what is occurring, look for someone who is better able to help you.

Another reason for broker/client breakdown is unrealistic expectations from the client or the broker. When the expectations are not met, disaster strikes. Be realistic. Be honest. Be decisive. And expect the exact same treatment from your broker. If you don't get it, take action because it is your money we're talking about.

In this chapter we have covered
— why have a stockbroker,
— how to find an appropriate broker,
— how to handle an interview with a prospective broker,
— what to expect at the end of your interview,
— what rules stockbrokers must follow,
— why client/broker relationships stop working.

If you're ready to proceed, we'll move on to the nuts and bolts of opening an account and to the specific documents and information you will receive from brokerage firms. There's lots still to know, but you have acquired a great deal of knowledge to this point. It's going to get very exciting from here on.

Chapter Five

INVESTMENT FIRMS AND STOCK EXCHANGES

Up until this point you have been preparing yourself. You have determined your past and present financial positions, and you have set your future goals. You have found and perhaps met with a stockbroker. You are now getting ready to test the waters where the financial action takes place.

Have you ever travelled to another country? If so, you know how it feels when you first arrive. You're a tourist and you're slightly disoriented. The more familiar you become with the lay of the land, the more you get to know the people and the language, the more confident you become. Meeting the market is a similar experience, for the market has its own history, customs, people, and language.

Let's survey the territory. The more you learn your way around, the more equipped you will be to assess various situations and accomplish your goals. Your stockbroker will be one of your guides.

BUT FIRST, A WORD ABOUT HOT TIPS
On the road to becoming a marketwise investor, you may be tempted to take one detour. *Don't do it*. Before I introduce you to the market, I must warn you about the wrong way to meet the market: hot tips.

How many times have I heard the same sad story? Lots and lots of normal people from every walk of life have been seduced by what they call hot tips.

The story goes like this: your hairdresser or your brother-in-law or the woman you meet walking your dog gives you information about a stock that is going to rise rapidly in price and make you a fortune. What you heard is, *you can't lose* if you invest in New Wave Enterprises or Cloud Nine Biotech or whatever the name of the hot-tip company may be.

Over and over again I have listened to the agonizing details of just how this "sure thing" became a loser. A short-term investment "guaranteed" to make money suddenly turned into useless pieces of nothing, which are being used as wallpaper in the bathroom several years later.

In my experience, the majority of hot tips are really lukewarm — highly-inflated exaggerations of rumours. Where the hot tip is not the product of an overactive imagination, it may be illegal. That's right. As the newspapers and press have shown us in detail over the last few years, *using inside information is a crime and crimes are punishable*.

Inside information is information which everyone does not have access to. Only the people working directly in or advising the company should know it. It is against the law for a company insider (such as a director) who knows what the company is planning to give out this information secretly or to act on or cause others to act on it for profit. It is a crime for insiders or for you to act on this information. The punishments I'm talking about are jail terms and severe fines. For stockbrokers who use this information, the penalties are even stronger. The Canadian Securities Commission, the body which licenses all stockbrokers, can suspend brokers' licenses and throw them out of the securities industry for a long, long time.

We must have laws which protect against the illegal use of information not available to everyone. Otherwise people would never invest in a stock market where the deck could be stacked against them so easily.

How to handle hot tips
If someone does give you a hot tip, here is a good way to respond:

1. Take a deep breath. (After all, every one of us probably dreams about a get-rich-quick scheme.)
2. Since the inside information is usually irrelevant, you ask the real juicy question: what price are the shares trading at today? For the sake of this example, let's say $2.00.
3. And what price are they going to rise to? $8.00. It sounds too good to be true.
4. Are you still buying more shares, you inquire. The response may be, "No, I own enough." How can any red-blooded, greedy individual ever say he or she owns enough of something which is "guaranteed" to go up four times from its current value? Until the price reaches $7.75, you do not own enough. Mortgage your house, sell your car, give up food, rent your children out, do anything to borrow the money because we are talking about riches you've only dreamt about.
5. To finalize this procedure, you next brazenly ask the person what price he or she paid for their shares? Hey, now is not the time to be shy. Sputter, sputter, cough, cough. If this tipster is on the level, he or she may tell you the truth. Let's say the answer is $0.25.
6. You now face a devilish dilemma. If this person is a friend, he or she could have told you about this hot tip sooner. You aren't greedy: a 700% profit — from $0.25 to $2.00 — would have suited you just fine. The dark side is if you buy these shares (which you know next to nothing about), they may well go back to $0.25. You will then face a loss of 88% of your money ($1.75 of the $2 you spent), but your "friend" will not have lost one penny. That is probably the only no-lose aspect of the story. The other no lose is if you take my advice and don't gamble on hot tips.

Hot Tips: A bad investment habit
There are many reasons why I do not like people to use hot tips, especially when they are first investing. First, taking such an action is usually a deviation from their financial objectives and strategies. Second, if the touted stock does go up and they make a profit, the stage has now been set for unrealistic expectations about what the market can do (remember I warned you about these in the last chapter). People can become over-confident, thinking that they understand the market completely and possess financial acumen. Not so, in most cases. And this first experience sets people up for a big fall later, when the stakes could be even higher.

Another reason is that if the hot tip does not work out, first-time investors get a sense of persecution. I hear statements such as "my mother told me not to get into the stock market, and she was right", and "I knew it was rigged and this just confirms my belief", and "the odds are always stacked against the little guy". These people now avoid the stock market for life and tell all their friends what a terrible place it is.

MY RECOMMENDED STRATEGY: *Avoid hot tips like the plague.* Professional traders who watch the market like hawks are plugged into some very important sources — how could they have missed this opportunity?

Truly successful investors don't use hot tips. Bernard Baruch, a millionaire at age 35 in 1905, says in his book, *Baruch — My Own Story*:

> Outside my office in Wall Street there used to be an old beggar to whom I often gave gratuities. One day during the 1929 madness he stopped me and said, "I have a good tip for you." When beggars and shoeshine boys, barbers and beauticians can tell you how to get rich, it is time to remind yourself that there is no more dangerous illusion than the belief that one can get something for nothing.

Let's get back to real investing.

WHY COMPANIES HAVE INVESTORS

From time to time corporations, large and small, must raise money in order to conduct business. The companies with the greatest ideas don't always have the greatest amount of cash to develop them. One way for firms to raise money is to "go public" — that is, to offer shares (partial ownership in the company) to the public (you and me). In essence, the company is willing to share the outcome of its activities with those people who have put up money to finance its operations. Investors give money to companies in the hope that they will eventually return the favour by providing the investors with income or, potentially, an increase in the value of their investment. These shareholders therefore become part owners of the companies.

THE MARKET FOR SECURITIES

How can investors know the fair price for their shares? The answer is that the prices of securities, like the prices of most goods and services in our economy, are set in the marketplace, which means, in broad terms, by supply and demand — what people are willing to sell and to buy for. In Canada, as in many countries, the activities of the market — the buying and selling — occur in two kinds of settings. The market for some securities is in *stock exchanges*, which are organized in specific places; the market for other securities is the *over-the-counter market*, which isn't a building at all but a network of buyers and sellers. Confused? Read on.

The stock exchange

On the most basic level, a stock exchange provides a marketplace for the buying and selling of securities. Stock exchanges are non-profit organizations that have members who own seats on the exchange and pay fees for the services they use.

Equity investing — buying and selling shares — is done on a stock exchange if a company is listed. Being *listed* means that the company has fulfilled various requirements set by the exchange (or exchanges) where it is listed and by the appropriate provincial securities commissions. (A company's stock can be de-listed for not continuing to meet the listing requirements.) A listing means the company's stock may be traded on that exchange and have the share prices put in the financial press. A listing on an exchange is not, however, a guarantee of the company's value as an investment.

The over-the-counter market

When people talk about the market, they tend to put stocks and bonds together, but, in fact, the two are traded in different places. Bonds and other debt instruments, such as Treasury bills and debentures, are traded over the counter (in broker talk, OTC) between dealers such as investment firms and financial institutions such as banks.

Some companies also have their shares traded OTC because they cannot or don't want to meet the listing requirements. These companies are called unlisted companies. Although many of the stocks trading OTC are stocks which trade for a few cents, some very reputable stocks, such as those of some insurance companies, are traded on the unlisted market, too. There is also NASDAQ (the National Association of Security Dealers), an "exchange" for buying and selling unlisted securities in the United States.

Therefore the stock market is different from the bond market. In fact, years ago, there were separate investment firms, some to handle stock trading and others for bond trading. Now most firms can handle all transactions, in stocks or bonds.

The reason for stock exchanges

As I said earlier, investors buy shares in companies in hope that these companies will eventually return the favour by providing them with income or growth or both. Companies issue certificates saying who is the owner of such-and-such a number of shares. But suppose an original owner wants to sell that certificate, and suppose people who didn't participate in the original issue want to buy now. What is needed is a forum where the securities can be traded for their fair market value, a place where one can find a buyer or a seller efficiently, make a transaction, and receive the best available price.

This is why a group of businessmen set up the Toronto Stock Exchange in 1852. Because the Toronto Stock Exchange (TSE) is Canada's biggest, I will concentrate on it in this book. Other North American stock exchanges work in similar fashion.

Investing for income or profit is why 7.4 billion shares were traded in 5.7 million separate transactions on the TSE in 1987. One hundred billion dollars was the value of shares traded in Canada in 1987 through the TSE. In addition to the TSE, there are four other exchanges across the country: the Montreal Exchange, the Alberta Stock Exchange (in Calgary), the Vancouver Stock Exchange, and the Winnipeg Commodities Exchange. Each exchange has its own rules and listing requirements. In this computer age, most brokers, in whichever province they are located, have access to all exchanges in order to get up-to-date prices and execute transactions for you.

If your city or even your province does not have a stock exchange, you can still buy and sell shares. You are governed by the rules of your provincial securities commission, and you must meet the investing requirements it sets down. Also, you can buy and sell securities on other exchanges in the world. (Some restrictions apply on various exchanges, so be sure to check them out before you take action.)

The TSE is not simply an elegant building gracing Toronto's downtown. The governors of the exchange are an appointed body that regulates and monitors the industry. The TSE has about 70 member firms, all part owners, and each must follow the rules of the exchange and of the securities commissions. These rules are to protect you, the investor. Because the industry is complex and the unwary could be taken advantage of, there are strict rules regulating the conduct of firms that are members of the exchange and of companies listed on it. Why? As I said earlier, if the public lacks confidence in the system, they will not invest their money, and then everyone loses.

For many the stock exchanges seem to be formidable, even forbidding places. Don't let them intimidate you. A mere 18% of Canadians invested their money in the market in 1986. A lack of knowledge and confidence has kept people from investing when investing might have been the most prudent thing to do with their money.

What does share ownership represent?
The 1085 companies listed on the TSE create jobs, explore and develop natural resources, research and develop products, manufacture goods, and provide services. When you purchase shares in, say, the Toronto-Dominion Bank, you are not simply buying a piece of paper. You are buying a piece of a company, with managers, employees, and a product. Yes, you are buying a piece of the action, but the action is the corporate fabric of the country. Your shares are more than just a piece of paper.

THE STOCK MARKET AND YOUR BROKER
With all these facts in mind, you are ready to make the next move in the investment area. You have your ally: your stockbroker.

You may ask why you can't do it all by yourself? You could. In fact when I first came into the investment industry, a woman asked me a very important question: "I know this is a dumb question, but I've always wanted to know if you have to sell your stock at the stock exchange." I laughed and told her that her question was so dumb that I didn't know the answer. But I did find out. You can trade with anyone without using the facilities of the stock exchange. All you have to do is find a buyer (or a seller), determine a fair price, and find a way for the buyer to know that the certificates are legitimate. This would be a *rare* situation. You could do most of these things, provided you are willing to invest sufficient time and energy. But it seems much easier to let the stock exchange do them for you.

In order to make a transaction on a stock exchange, you need to deal with a member of the stock exchange. You can't just walk down to the stock exchange and place an order. You must place the order with a firm which holds a seat on the exchange where you wish to make a transaction.

Brokers are employees of the member firms that hold seats on the exchange. Having a seat on the exchange allows the firm to make transactions on the floor of the exchange on behalf of its customers.

Full-service brokerage firms
The major services of a full-service firm (sometimes called a fully integrated firm) include offering to transact business for financial products and services (including stocks, bonds, options, and registered retirement savings plans), providing corporate financial services, and offering research opinions.

Some brokers make a lot of money, but they are not all millionaires. They make money by charging a commission, typically 2 to 2.5% of the value of the trade of amounts less than $25,000 and less than 2% on larger trades. The investment firm keeps much of the commission in exchange for providing the broker with everything needed to do business — a research department, trading capabilities, a phone, a desk, an assistant, and so on. Each firm has a minimum commission, generally ranging from $40 to $70. Most firms do not have minimum transaction levels or minimum accounts. So theoretically you could start with a small amount of money and buy just one share. But remember the commission — the minimum charge — could leave you paying more in costs than you pay for your investment.

What should you expect from your broker in exchange for your fee? Time, information, service, and the efficient execution of all the orders you place, plus a prompt record of all of your activities on a monthly statement. I have already noted, quoting from the book *Megatrends*, that we are drowning in information but starved for knowledge. What you really pay a broker for is the knowledge to take you through everything in an efficient manner. Any information you receive from a stockbroker could be found somewhere. But how long would it take you to find it and do you have the know-how to look for it and see how it could be valuable?

The research department
Another important ally to have is the research department at the brokerage firm. Each corporation issues information. That's a lot of paper and numbers. With all this material available, it can be useful to have someone examine it from an objective (investor-oriented) perspective. This is where the research department comes in.

Some brokerage firms are known for their research abilities. When you first call a sales manager, you can ask whether the firm has research staff. Most do. If you are interested in a particular area of the market — such as media stocks — note which firms employ the expert analysts who are quoted in the newspaper. These analysts spend all of their days looking at specific industries. This means examining the companies' financial statements and competitors' financial statements, seeing what's happening in the industry as a whole and what's happening in the market and the economy, and considering political and social influences on these stocks.

YOUR INVESTMENT ACCOUNT
Once you decide that you and your prospective stockbroker have a meeting of financial minds, the next step is to set up an account. There is paperwork to be completed to comply with securities legislation. Your broker will begin by asking for more confidential information on your financial affairs. It is not that he or she is nosey. Rather the securities commissions require the broker to obtain this information in order to ensure that you are in a position to invest, both legally and monetarily. To open an independent brokerage account, you must be of a certain age and have certain assets. (Both figures vary from province to province.)

EXHIBIT 5.1
A Typical Account Form

ACCOUNT EXECUTIVE'S NAME	AE CODE	ACCOUNT NUMBER

LANGUAGE OF ACCOUNT	☐ ENGLISH	☐ FRENCH

CUSTOMER'S NAME/Mr. Mrs. Ms. Miss

MAILING ADDRESS

POSTAL CODE

CURRENCY OF ACCOUNT	TYPE OF ACCOUNT	HOME ADDRESS
☐ CANADIAN FUNDS	☐ CASH ☐ RRSP	
☐ U.S. FUNDS	☐ COD ☐ ISIP	POSTAL CODE
	☐ MARGIN ☐ QSSP	
OTHER	☐ SHORT MARGIN	

TYPE OF OPTIONS TRADING - if any - (TRADE CODE)

☐ COVERED WRITING (2)	☐ SPREADING (3)	BUSINESS PHONE	HOME PHONE
☐ BUYING (1)	☐ NAKED WRITING (4)	SOCIAL INSURANCE NO.	APPROX. AGE	DEPENDENTS

SPOUSE'S NAME	SPOUSE'S EMPLOYER	EMPLOYER'S NAME
SPOUSE'S OCCUPATION	SPOUSE'S TYPE OF BUSINESS	TYPE OF BUSINESS	POSITION HELD

CUSTOMER'S OVERALL INVESTMENT OBJECTIVES	RISK FACTORS	
	☐ Investment Grade	NET LIQUID ASSETS (Cash and securities less loans outstanding against securities)
☐ Income	☐ Good Quality	
☐ Growth (Inter Term)	☐ Speculative	
☐ Growth (Long Term)	☐ High Risk	NET FIXED ASSETS (Fixed assets less liabilities outstanding against fixed assets)

CUSTOMER'S PAST INVESTMENT EXPERIENCE

☐ Stocks ☐ Options ☐ Bonds	TOTAL NET WORTH
☐ Short Sales ☐ Commodities ☐ Other	
Most money in the market at any one time $	APPROXIMATE ANNUAL INCOME FROM ALL SOURCES

ACCOUNTS WITH OTHER BROKERAGE FIRMS:

CREDIT REFERENCE (MGR. MUST INITIAL IF WAIVED)

RELATED ACCOUNT NUMBERS ☐ NO ☐ YES	BANK NAME
(LIST)	
NAMES OF PUBLIC COMPANIES IN WHICH CUSTOMER IS AN OFFICER OR DIRECTOR:	BANK BRANCH
	PERSON CONTACTED
NAMES OF PUBLIC COMPANIES IN WHICH CUSTOMER OWNS OR CONTROLS 10% OR MORE OF VOTING RIGHTS:	INITIAL DEPOSIT	INITIAL ORDER
	(MANAGER MUST INITIAL IF WAIVED)	
DOES ANYONE OTHER HAVE AUTHORITY OR ANY FINANCIAL INTEREST IN THE ACCOUNT: ☐ NO ☐ YES (LIST)		

HOW LONG HAVE YOU KNOWN THE CUSTOMER?	TRADE LIMITS (if any)
☐ PHONE/WALK IN ☐ ADVERTISING LEAD	TRADE RESTRICTIONS
☐ PERSONAL CONTACT	ACCOUNT EXECUTIVE'S SIGNATURE DATE
☐ KNOWN PERSONALLY	
REFERRAL BY	BRANCH MANAGER'S OR ALTERNATE'S APPROVAL DATE
DUPLICATE CONFIRMATIONS TO:	
	DESIGNATED DIRECTOR'S APPROVAL DATE
	DESIGNATED REGISTERED OPTIONS PRINCIPAL'S APPROVAL DATE

Merrill Lynch Canada Inc.

Exhibit 5.1 is a typical account form, one used by Merrill Lynch financial consultants with their clients. Fill it in, as a reminder for later years of your starting point.
Also, having done this exercise will leave you well prepared for meeting your stockbroker because you'll have thought about your answers carefully. You can open several types of accounts. Most people open a cash account or a margin account.

Cash Accounts

A *cash account* is straightforward. You ask your broker to complete a transaction for you, and then you pay for your securities (in the case of a purchase) or you receive money (in the case of a sale). The stockbroker's commission is calculated with your transaction. On a regular transaction, you pay for your purchase or receive money from your sale in five business days.

Margin Accounts

What if you want to buy $10,000 worth of stocks but don't have that much money?
A *margin account* is an account which lets you borrow money from the investment firm. Stocks trading at a price of $2 or more per share are marginable at 50%, meaning that the brokerage firm is allowed to loan you 50% of the price the stock is trading at.
When you make your purchase, you can pay half of the amount owed, and the brokerage firm will lend you the other half, charging you interest on the amount you borrow.
The annual rate is somewhat above prime rate (often prime plus 2 percentage points), and this interest is charged monthly. Remember to check all these details when you open your account. Some investment firms have their own, more stringent requirements for margin trading, so be sure to ask before you assume.

To show you exactly how a margin account works, here's an example.

Say you buy 100 shares at $20 per share for a value of $2000. Forget the commission for the moment. You put up $1000, and the firm loans you $1000 and charges you interest on the money you borrow. This is your margin.

Now what happens? In the worst case scenario, the stock goes down, let's say to $18. Initially you were loaned $1000, but now the firm, which must stick to the 50%-margin rule, can advance only $900 (50% × $18 = $9). You receive what is known as a margin call. You must come up with the extra $100 ($1000 − $900). If you do not come forward with the necessary margin — by selling some of your stocks, by bringing in more stocks as collateral, or by bringing in the cash — the firm must sell some of your stocks to bring you "on side" (meaning that you meet the margin requirements).

Margin is one of those ideas that is great when it's going right, and murder when it is going wrong. It is another of the seesaw reactions which occur in investments.

In our example, you have lost 20% of your money if you have to sell. (You put up $1000 for shares that were worth $2000 and are worth only $1800 now.) Horrible. But what if it had gone the other way?

In the best case scenario, the stock goes up, let's say to $22. You now have an investment worth $2200. If you sell today, you will have made 20% on your money (you will receive $1200 after paying off your margin debt, and you originally invested $1000). You're in great shape.

Of course, these calculations do not take into account commission or interest charges, but you get the basic idea. When people speak of *leverage*, they are referring to putting up a limited amount of money and borrowing the rest in hopes of making a greater percentage return than if the whole amount were originally paid in full. Buying the stock for $2000 and selling at $2200 would have only provided a 10% return on your money ($200 profit on $2000 invested). On margin, as we saw, the same increase provided a 20% return ($200 profit on $1000 invested).

If you are fortunate and the stock goes up, then the brokerage firm will carry you (and charge interest) until you sell the stock. In our risk-and-reward review, you are risking having to put up more money for margin but you have the potential to make more money on the amount you've invested.

MY RECOMMENDED STRATEGY: If you are going to use margin, don't borrow close to the margin limit. Keep a cushion of money between you and a margin call, just in case the stock fluctuates and you need that extra amount. When the stock markets took a swift decline on October 19, 1987, dropping 20 to 30%, many margin calls were issued.

BEFORE YOU PLACE YOUR FIRST ORDER

Let's say you have opened an account. Your broker cannot initiate a transaction without your specific instructions. Unless you have set up a special — and rare — kind of account known as a discretionary account, every trade you make has to be authorized by you. (A discretionary account is one in which you sign an authorization for a partner or director of a brokerage firm to make trading decisions on your behalf without consulting you first. You are informed after the fact.) You cannot authorize a trade in another person's account, even your spouse's, unless you and that person have signed a trading authorization.

Before you make your first purchase, the firm may ask you to deposit a few hundred dollars in your account before you buy (the request could even be for more, depending on the size of the purchases you contemplate). If you are selling, the firm may ask you to deposit the shares you wish to sell before the sell order is placed. This happens only on the first transaction, in order to generate goodwill on each side. Because you do not have to pay for a stock transaction (or receive money if you sell) for five business days after the trade, you can see why a firm might justifiably take these steps.

HOW TO PLACE AN ORDER

A basic building block in becoming an investor is knowing how to place an order. You don't want to make a mistake in this crucial area. There are 17 possible types of orders, some with exotic names such as "fill or kill" and "all or none". Large institutional investors place all types of orders, but for you and me two types of orders are enough: market orders and limit orders.

Market orders

When you give a *market order*, you mean that the shares should be bought or sold at the current market price. You may call your broker and ask what price Bell Canada Enterprises is trading at. The answer, which will take the form of a quotation, will go something like: 39¼ to 39½. Notice that the price of shares trading at $5 or more is quoted with fractional amounts in eighths of a dollar (⅛ of $1 = 12.5 cents).

On the left of the quotation is the *bid price*, 39¼, which means the price that investors are willing to pay per share for 100 shares. One hundred shares is a *board lot*, the standard trading unit for shares traded at $1 or more, just as a dozen eggs is the standard unit for buying eggs. It would be inefficient to offer a price on 1 and 9 and 468 shares, so the unit is standardized.

On the right side of the quotation is the *ask price*, also known as the offered price. Here it is 39½. This figure stands for what investors are currently willing to sell 100 shares for per share.

Bid and ask prices are updated continuously throughout trading hours. Because the amounts change during the day, you hear reports in the media discussing the opening price (the first trade for that stock for the day), the closing price (the last price paid in the day), and various high and low prices established as trading continues throughout the day. Price changes occur because of news, because of supply and demand by investors, and because of general market sentiment.

EXHIBIT 5.2
An Order Ticket

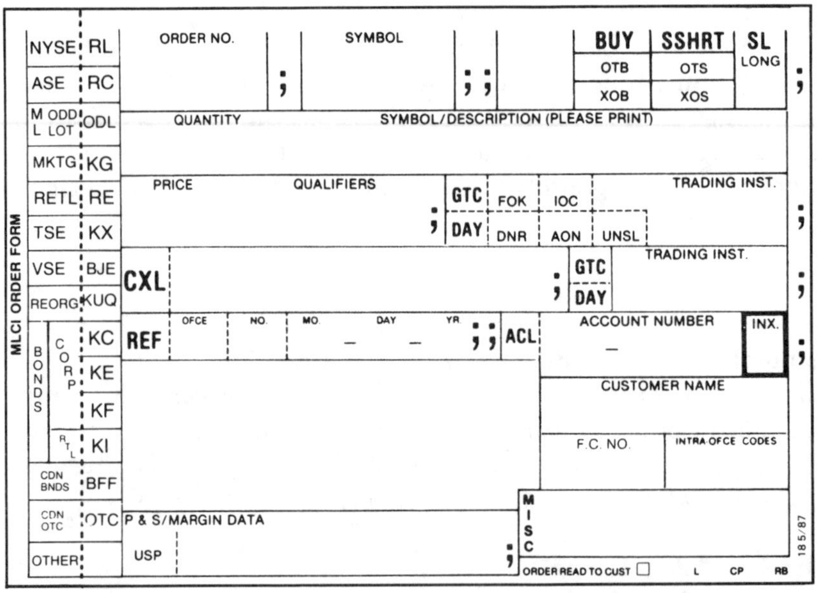

Merrill Lynch Canada Inc.

If you tell your broker to buy or sell at market, he or she fills out the order on a "ticket" (see Exhibit 5.2), verifies it with you, takes it to the trading desk or wire room, which calls or wires the firm's floor traders (at the exchange where the shares are traded), who then execute your order at the best possible price at that moment. When the order is completed, the floor traders report back to the trading desk, and the information is passed on to the stockbroker and ultimately to you. As you can see, a lot of people are needed to complete orders, even in our computer age.

Limit orders
The *limit order* is the other major trading order. In this case, you call your broker and

ask for the quotation. You place a limit order, which is an order to buy (or sell) a specific stock at a specific price.

You give a limit order because you have set certain criteria for your investing. For example, you may ask your broker to buy 100 shares of Superinvestor Company stock at $39 limit even though the shares are trading at $45 today. You also set a time frame for this order: just for today, for this week, or for this month you are willing to take that many shares at that price. Remember your word is gospel on this. Your broker repeats the order back to you to confirm it; you will also receive a notification in the mail reminding you of the details of the order.

While the order is outstanding, you can phone and cancel it. If your broker calls with a ''fill'', it means that you have obtained the shares at the price you wanted. At that point you cannot say you have changed your mind. Remember, your word is gospel.

You can, of course, withdraw an order that has not yet been filled. But if you place limit orders and each time the price starts to near your order, you phone to change your mind, you are likely to come to the end of your relationship with your broker. You must ask yourself why you picked that price in the first place. I find this a standard mistake which newer investors make. They want to buy stock cheaper than the current price, but when it declines to near their price, they get scared.

When your order has been completed
Every time you make a transaction you will receive a *confirmation* with the details of the trade (see Exhibit 5.3). It shows your trade date (when the order was filled) and your settlement date (when you must pay money if you purchased or will receive money if you sold). It also tells you which security it represents, which account you traded it in, how much you bought or sold at what price, and how much commission was paid. Finally, it tells you the total cost of or net proceeds from the transaction.

EXHIBIT 5.3
A Confirmation

Merrill Lynch Canada Inc.

EXHIBIT 5.4
A Sample Monthly Statement

YOUR FINANCIAL CONSULTANT	OFFICE SERVING YOUR ACCOUNT	
JOHN SMITH (416) 586-6000 AA	MERRILL LYNCH CANADA 200 KING ST. W., TORONTO, ONT. M5H 3W3	MR. CHARLES M. ACCOUNT 1234 MAIN STREET ANYWHERE ONTARIO M1M 1M1
STATEMENT PERIOD FROM 09/25/87 TO 10/30/87	PAGE 1 OF 3	

YOUR ACCOUNTS

20-047A-1   CASH   CDN.   20-047E-1   MGN   CDN.   20-451F-2   MGN   U.S.

THE CONVERSION RATE FOR THIS STATEMENT PERIOD IS $1.35 CANADIAN FOR EACH U.S. DOLLAR.

FINANCIAL SUMMARY

Account	Type	Funds	Opening Balance	Closing Balance	Market Value	Equity
20-047A-1	CASH	CDN.	931.98CR	976.36CR	1,699.00CR	2,675.36CR
20-047E-1	MGN	CDN.	26,291.73	109,943.07	343,825.00CR	233,881.93CR
20-451F-2	MGN	U.S.	2,589.32	2,615.77	20,000.00CR	17,384.23CR
CANADIAN ACCOUNTS			$25,359.75	$108,966.71	$345,524.00CR	$236,557.29CR
U.S. ACCOUNTS			$2,589.32	$2,615.77	$20,000.00CR	$17,384.23CR
TOTAL IN CANADIAN FUNDS			$28,655.33	$112,498.00	$372,524.00CR	$260,026.00CR

DIVIDENDS AND INTEREST

Account	Type	Funds	Interest This Month Debit	Interest This Month Credit	Interest Year To Date Debit	Interest Year To Date Credit	Dividends This Month	Dividends Year To Date
20-047A-1	CASH	CDN.	0.00	8.21	0.00	8.21	36.17CR	36.17CR
20-047E-1	MGN	CDN.	184.78	0.00	184.78	0.00	285.00CR	285.00CR
20-451F-2	MGN	U.S.	26.45	0.00	26.45	0.00	0.00	0.00
CANADIAN ACCOUNTS			$184.78	$8.21	$184.78	$8.21	$321.17CR	$321.17CR
U.S. ACCOUNTS			$26.45	$0.00	$26.45	$0.00	$0.00	$0.00
TOTAL IN CANADIAN FUNDS			$220.49	$8.21	$220.49	$8.21	$321.17CR	$321.17CR

ACTIVITIES THIS MONTH

Date	Bought/Received	Sold/Delivered	Description	Price / Entry	Amount	Balance
20-047A-1 CASH CDN.						
09/25			OPENING BALANCE			931.98CR
10/16			INT OCT 16	INTEREST	8.21CR	
10/16	200		INTL THOM ORG-CUM THOM BR	DIVIDEND	36.17CR	976.36CR
10/30			CLOSING BALANCE			976.36CR
20-047E-1 MGN CDN.						
09/25			OPENING BALANCE			26,291.73
10/05			PER REQ	CHEQUE ISSUED	1,000.00	
10/05	55,000		HIR WALKER W/WB.5%15JAN94	100.000	55,000.00	82,291.73
10/09		300	FIRST CITY FINL CORP LTD	23.000	6,762.00CR	75,529.73
10/13		700	FIRST CITY FINL CORP LTD	23.000	15,791.72CR	59,738.01
10/14	1,000		ROMAN CORPORATION LTD	9.250	9,510.00	69,248.01
10/15	1,000		FIRST CITY FINL CORP LTD	DIVIDEND	125.00CR	69,123.01
10/16			INT TO OCT 16 @ 12.00%	INTEREST	466.56	69,589.57
10/19	500		STRATHEARN HOUSE GR-A-NVS	2.090	0.00	
10/19	4,500		STRATHEARN HOUSE GR-A-NVS	2.100	10,823.20	80,412.77
10/20	2,000		AUTOMOTIVE HARDWARE CL A	14.500	29,530.30	109,943.07
10/30			CLOSING BALANCE			109,943.07
20-451F-2 MGN U.S.						
09/25			OPENING BALANCE			2,589.32
10/16			INT TO OCT 16 @ 11.00%	INTEREST	26.45	2,615.77
10/30			CLOSING BALANCE			2,615.77

SECURITY POSITIONS

Long	Short	Security Description	Price	Market Value	Segregated	Safekeeping
20-047A-1 CASH CDN.						
1,000		COMTERM INC	1.300	1,300.00	1,000	
700		TRINITY RESOURCES LTD	0.570	399.00		700
20-047E-1 MGN CDN.						
10,000		AGASSIZ RESOURCES LTD	3.700	37,000.00		
2,000		AUTOMOTIVE HARDWARE CL A	14.500	29,000.00		
1,000		BNK OF MTL $2.50 PR - A	27.500	27,500.00		
7,500		CADILLAC FAIRVIEW PRF-A	9.875	74,062.50		
1,000		CDA DEVEL CRP$2.35 SEN PF	25.125	25,125.00		
500		GENSTAR CRP$2.35CV 2ND PF	27.375	13,687.50		
500		IVACO INC SUB CL A VTG SH	21.750	10,875.00		
2,400		NORTHERN TELECOM LTD	41.000	98,400.00		
1,000		OAKWOOD PETE-CL A NON VTG	1.700	1,700.00		
1,000		ROMAN CORPORATION LTD	9.375	9,375.00		
10,000		STRATHEARN HOUSE GR-A-NVS	1.710	17,100.00		
20-451F-2 MGN U.S.						
1,000		ALASKA AIRLINES	20.000	20,000.00		

TRANSACTIONS TO SETTLE AFTER 10/30/87

Date	Bought/Received	Sold/Delivered	Description	Price / Entry	Amount
20-047E-1 MGN CDN.					
11/06	100		CARA OPERATIONS	12.000	1,200.00

For the purpose of this example, the statement has been reduced to one page.

Merrill Lynch Canada Inc.

In addition to this confirmation, you will receive a monthly statement such as the one in Exhibit 5.4 (I wish that portfolio was mine!). It states all these details plus others, such as interest charges on your account or interest paid to you. It is important that you read these documents as soon as they arrive and that you save them with your important records in your expanding A–Z file. You will need this information at tax time.

We're going to look more closely at what's in your best tax interest as well as at tax products in a later chapter. For the moment, remember that your broker is not licensed to give tax advice. Lawyers and accountants are able to do this. (When you see tax information from a brokerage firm, a lawyer or an accountant has prepared it.) But again, as you've heard me say and will continue to hear me say, it's your money, so you must stay on top of your tax situation. If you have a broker and an accountant or a lawyer, make sure that they are all working as a team to assist you in the direction that best suits your needs. Your advisors aren't (or shouldn't be) in competition with each other; they should be working in co-operation to assist you. Don't hesitate to have your lawyer or accountant speak to your broker or vice versa.

AFTER YOU HAVE BOUGHT A STOCK

You have established your goals and understand various strategies can take you there. After the meeting with your broker, you have agreed on a course of action. You have bought something. If you have a long-term strategy, you do not need to call your broker every day to check on it. This will waste everybody's time and cause you undue anxiety. Calling every day to find out the price of various securities has to be close to the top of the list of investor mistakes. If you don't intend to sell, just review the price in the newspaper. Exhibit 5.5 shows you how.

EXHIBIT 5.5
How to Read Newspaper Listings

Year High	Low	Stock	Div	High	Low	Close	Change	Vol
$ 17	$14-3/4	Acme T. & D.	$ 72	$16-3/4	$16-1/8	$16-1/8	-5/8	400
29-3/8	26	Comput Co.	2.28	29-1/4	29-1/4	29-1/4	-1/8	100
15	7-7/8	O & G Expl. A		9	8-3/4	8-7/8	-1/8	14400
8	490	Vn. Mining		5-1/2	5-1/2	5-1/2	-1/8 z	20
3/4	26-1/2	Sec. Bank	2.00	27	26-1/2	27	+1/4	19625
345	2	Alpha Oil		280	270	280	-5	30500
15-1/4	7-1/2	Imp Trus	1.20	13-1/2	12-1	13-1/4	-1	64353
5-1/4	350	West Ont ach		400	400	400	+25	205
24-1/4	15-1/2	UNI C	90	21-3/4	17-1/8	21-3/4	+2-3/4	24480
2-5/8	39-1/8	C F n Ent	2.05	42-3/4	41-1/2	42-5/8	+3/8	9087-4
31	24	Ke ra Iron	1.70	27	26-3/4	27	+1/2	908
23-1/2	19-1/4	Silv Tel	1.45	22-1/4	21-1/8	21-3/4	+1/4	17038
10-1/4	8-1/2	wood Pkg		9-1/2	9-3/8	9-1/2	-1/8	1600
11-1/2	7-3/4	Gamma Res		9-5/8	9-1/8	9-3/8	-1/8	9724
175	75	SYNBLEND Pr		140	108	13	+8	76200
310	20	IBL Br		275	220	268		27600
150	146-1/2	Lon Util	3.15	149-1/4	147-3/4	149-1/4	+1-1/2	344

1. Highest and lowest price paid for the stock to date this year. Venture Mining stock has traded as high as $8.00, and as low as $4.90 during the year. Shares traded under $5.00 are quoted in cents.

2. Abbreviated name of the company issuing the stock. This listing refers to Oil and Gas Exploration Limited's Class 'A' stock.

3. Annual dividend paid by the company. This is a projected annual rate based on dividend payments over the last twelve months.

4. Highest price paid for the stock during this trading session was $16-3/4, and the lowest was $16-1/8.

5. Price paid for the last board lot traded was $27.00. This was up 1/4 or 25 cents from the closing price in the previous session.

6. Number of shares traded during the trading session. The symbol z indicates that less than a board lot traded.

Toronto Stock Exchange

If you see the price of a stock decline by 50 cents or a dollar, do not panic. You bought it for the long term, remember? One of the best analogies I ever heard about this phenomenon was from a broker I used to work with. He would ask nervous investors whether their house was their biggest investment. Right, they would answer. Then he asked if they went out on their front lawn every day to determine the price saying, "Today it's sunny and looking good, $250,000." If the next day wasn't so good, only $240,000. Did they sell the next day at $240,000? No, of course not. So they shouldn't think of selling their stocks because they had fluctuated in price either. Just because stock prices are listed in the paper every day, some investors have a tendency to watch them overzealously. Don't do it. You will drive yourself and your broker crazy and for no good reason.

When to call your stockbroker

You can expect calls from your broker, recommending investments suitable for your needs. If you have found a security you are considering for investment, by all means, ask your broker about it. Also call your broker when you have a question. General questions are best discussed before or after market hours, which are currently 9:30 a.m. to 4:00 p.m. Eastern Standard Time not only for the Toronto, Montreal, and New York stock exchanges, but also for those in Alberta and Vancouver. You can decide when to call in the case of a specific transaction you wish to make during market hours.

If you think this advice sounds funny, put yourself in the broker's position. He or she makes money by buying and selling securities, and this can be done only between 9:30 a.m. and 4:00 p.m. Imagine you are a storeowner. What if someone comes into your store six times a day, never purchases anything, but keeps you from talking to potential customers. You are understandably annoyed. I am not discouraging you from calling your broker. My message is simply that you will receive better treatment from the broker if you think a little about his or her time constraints before you pick up the phone.

MY RECOMMENDED STRATEGY: Ask general questions before or after market hours and discuss transaction questions during market hours.

What if your stockbroker is away

If your broker is on holiday or away for a day when you wish to place an order, you can speak to his or her assistant. That person is usually licensed to handle the transaction for you. Alternatively, your broker may have arranged for another broker in the office to cover for this period. The other broker won't be as familiar with your account, but he or she can certainly take your order and execute it.

Keep informed

I recommend that you do work on your own to learn more about the investment world. Ask your broker to recommend books on investing, or to make specific suggestions for reading material relevant to your portfolio. Ask to be put on mailing lists for appropriate material. See Chapter Eleven for some of my suggestions.

Minding your money

No industry is composed entirely of saints, and the brokerage business is no exception. Here are a few areas to watch out for and some hints on how to prevent problems.

The first possible problem is *churning*, the industry name for excessive trading of securities in and out of your account just to generate commissions. "Excessive" is a judgement call; therefore you can prevent this by setting guidelines with your broker right at the beginning. Tell your broker you are a long-term investor (if that is what you are) and that moving in and out of securities is not your strategy. If, on the other hand, you want to trade the market price movements up and down, tell your broker this also. Only you can determine how often is too often, but coming to an understanding with your broker right at the start is the key to avoiding future problems.

Another problem area is what to do if you are losing money by taking your broker's advice. Ask these questions before you give up on your broker: how long have you given the broker to implement your strategy? have you given it enough time? has the entire market performed poorly, and not just your stocks? Investing is a matter of setting goals to be achieved over time — so don't become impatient and lose sight of your longer-term strategy. I know many people have given up too soon, and I don't want to see you lose out this way.

In *The Money Masters*, author John Train quotes Warren Buffett: "You must have the security and self-confidence that comes from knowledge, without being rash or headstrong. If you lack confidence, fear will drive you out at the bottom."

When *should* you become concerned? If your broker does not return your phone calls, if you don't receive the transaction confirmations promptly, or if your broker's recommendations are not consistent with the firm's recommendations. (The firm's recommendations are listed in its research publications.) These are all flags which should make you extra cautious.

If you are concerned, ask the broker what is going on. If you aren't satisfied with the answer, phone the branch manager. As a last resort, you can contact the provincial securities commission, but matters rarely get to this point. Brokerage firms are businesses, and they want to keep clean records. They do not want any wrongdoing with your portfolio any more than you do. In fact, brokers rarely require external discipline because several in-house checking systems are in place to detect irregularities. Even so, and I know I keep saying this, it is your money and so you must look out for it.

Why stockbrokers want you as a client
Stockbrokers want to have a long-term relationship with you. They realize the importance of having you as a valued client for many years. They want to be your financial consultant for 20 to 30 years. They are going to try their best to help you execute your strategy and reach your goals. They want you to attain your goals because then you will be a satisfied customer, and you will stay with them and continue to provide them with business. The more money you make, the more you have to invest. Also, if you are happy, you will refer other people to your broker because of the superior advice and service you have received. This is how stockbrokers increase their business.

In this chapter we covered
  — hot tips,
  — the stock exchanges and the over-the-counter markets,
  — investment firms,
  — setting up an account,
  — placing orders with confidence,
  — what to do after you buy.

Now you have the details on the arenas where stock and bond transactions happen and how to act in them. Your stockbroker will provide you with information about and opportunities to invest in various securities. You need to understand these products to determine whether or not they can help you reach your goals. So we are now ready to survey what I refer to as the Banquet Table of Investment Choices and to learn the specifics about stocks, bonds, and all the other securities available to you.

Chapter Six

PAYING YOU BACK WITH INTEREST: INTEREST-BEARING INVESTMENTS

So now that you have your approach to investments in perspective, what do you invest in? This is what we have all been waiting for — action.

When considering investments, I like to put all of the choices out on what I call the Banquet Table. Viewing investments on a Banquet Table, you realize that there are many choices. There are also many places you can start. There is no specific order. You can choose to participate by sampling a number of investments from the table or by selecting just one. You can also choose to step back and not take anything. There is no specific routine. Your investment choices are personal and suited just to you.

You do, however, want to remember the value of diversification. Smart investors don't trap themselves, putting all their eggs in one basket. This is why asset mix is so important. You want to build towards having investments in more than one area so that you will never be totally exposed, risking an absolute win or loss with your money.

Most Canadians are conservative investors who sock their hard-earned money away into savings accounts, Canada Savings Bonds (CSBs), and term deposits, such as certificates of deposit (CDs) and guaranteed investment certificates (GICs). In fact, surveys indicate that a large percentage of Canadians make no investments other than interest-bearing investments, registered retirement savings plans, and their homes.

Since interest-bearing investments are such popular investments and the types available have expanded so much in recent years, let's examine them and see if they could be valuable to you. These are the instruments that generally fall under the regular income objective of your investment strategy.

DEBT INSTRUMENTS
Savings accounts, GICs, and bonds all have one feature in common: the payment of interest. You loan your money, receive interest for a period of time, and eventually get your original investment back. Any investments in which you loan money to a company or a government and expect interest paid in return are called *debt instruments* or *debt investments*.

Many people choose these investments for their interest income and for the comfort of owning what are generally considered the most secure products available.

THE SPREAD
We both know that no company can operate without making money, so how do banks and trust companies make money when you buy a term deposit or put funds in a savings account? They make money on *the spread*, which is the difference between the rate of interest they pay you to borrow your money and the rate of interest they charge someone who borrows from them.

If you are paid 6% interest and someone else takes out a loan and is charged 11%, the 5% difference is the spread. Let's put this 5% figure into perspective with a $10,000 example.

$10,000 at 11% to borrower = $1100 interest charge
$10,000 at 6% to lender = $600 interest payment
Spread = $500 to the financial institution

The financial institution uses this $500 to pay the salaries of the employees who process the borrowing and lending transactions. It also must pay all the expenses of operating the buildings where people go to make these transactions. And it would like to make a profit.

In addition the banks and trust companies have a major responsibility. If you are a lender, you must be paid, whether or not the borrower makes good on his loan repayment. When you go to collect the *principal* (the original amount you loaned) on your term deposit, the bankers can't say, "Sorry, we loaned money to a foreign country and it missed a payment. Come back tomorrow and try again." Basically, the financial institutions run the risk of having someone default on a loan while they still have an obligation to pay you, the lender. In our world of facts, risk, and reward, these financial giants face decisions very similar to the ones we face.

Interest rates are of vital importance to bankers, borrowers, and savers alike. Investors must monitor interest rates in order to stay on top of their investment strategy. For years interest rates remained at about 4%, and then in the 1970s they began to increase and fluctuate.

BONDS AND DEBENTURES

Bonds and debentures are certificates you get when you loan your money to an organization such as a corporation or the government. The bond or debenture indicates the amount of money you have loaned, on which you will receive interest. The organization which gave you this bond or debenture also agrees to repay you the original amount loaned to them on a stipulated date, called the *maturity date*, which is shown on the bond. Unlike CSBs and term deposits, bonds and debentures can be traded again and again on the over-the-counter (OTC) market.

There are two general categories of bonds: government and corporate. We'll look at government bonds first.

Government bonds

Canada Savings Bonds, which we discussed in Chapter 1, are a special type of government bond. There are many others issued by municipal, provincial, and federal governments. Each is guaranteed by the applicable government body. The interest they pay is calculated at an annual rate but paid every six months. Bonds are generally issued in lots of $1000 (some are issued in lots of $100,000, too), but the price in the newspaper is quoted in $100 amounts.

Bonds are issued in varying maturities. One-year, three-year, five-year, and 15-year bonds are standard. There is more risk in taking a longer maturity, so naturally the 15-year bond generally has the highest interest rate of the four. A long-term bond is riskier than a short-term bond because inflation, interest rates, and various other economic factors could come into play long before it matures. You can't predict exactly what will happen. To compensate for this risk, you want a higher rate of interest.

If you listened to brokers discussing bonds, you might hear one of them say, "What is the level on the GOC 9½s of 2001?" This translates into "What is approximately the most recent trading price (level) of the Government of Canada (GOC) bonds which have a 9½% coupon (the annual interest rate payable on a $1000 bond) and which are due (coming to maturity, which means the holder will receive the $1000 back for each bond and no more interest payments will be made) on October 1, 2001?". . . . Once again, when you know the language, it's easy.

Corporate bonds

Companies issue corporate bonds in order to raise money without having to go to the bank for a loan. The bonds are generally guaranteed by a specific asset of the company, such as its buildings or inventory.

Because corporations cannot offer as much security as many governments, corporate bonds have to give higher rates of interest to compensate you for the risk you are taking.

Companies also issue *debentures*, which are much the same as bonds but generally offer the investor less protection since bondholders get paid before debenture holders if the company runs into financial problems. This difference in repayment rankings can make a difference if the company is in financial trouble.

Convertible bonds and debentures

Convertible bonds and debentures are a sort of cross between stocks and bonds. They pay a rate of interest lower than that of a non-convertible corporate bond or debenture. As compensation, they give you as the holder the option to convert your certificate into common shares of the company for a certain time period. What you give up today is some certain amount of current interest income. In exchange, you get an instrument with the potential for capital growth if the company prospers, the common shares rise in price, and you sell your certificate or convert it into shares.

We'll discuss convertibles more in the next chapter since they are really more stock market vehicles than interest-bearing vehicles.

Bond ratings

There is an elaborate rating system, like report cards, for all bonds, ranging from triple A (the best) down to C, or, in the worst case, no rating. These ratings classify bonds in terms of their credit risk and security as an investment. Your broker can tell you the rating for just about any bond you're considering. These ratings are obtained from one of the two major private bond-rating services: the Dominion Bond Rating Service and the Canadian Bond Rating Service.

The rating reflects the perception of the riskiness of the bond and, for corporate bonds, in some ways the profitability or potential of the company. The rating is important to know since it reflects the ability of the issuer to pay you the interest you are owed. For the investor, another significance is that a bond with a lower rating, say, a B or C, pays a higher rate of interest than a triple A bond. More risk is associated with a lower rating, and therefore the issuer of the bond must pay a higher rate of interest to compensate investors for taking that risk. Federal government bonds tend to be rated triple A because the bond-rating service knows that the Government of Canada can pay back the money. Governments are the best credit risk because they can tax us in order to raise the money they need. (I know this may be a simplistic way of looking at the matter, but you get the point.)

Corporate bonds do not get as high a rating as government bonds. Some blue-chip companies with good track records for growth and payment of debts, such as Bell Canada Enterprises, get high ratings on their bonds. Others, such as some natural resource companies, get lower ratings.

Buying bonds

Attracting money is a competitive business. The preparers of these offerings on the Banquet Table have to calculate how to best attract takers. The issuers of bonds, debentures, and other interest-bearing certificates must offer a competitive rate of interest. It is the competitive rate which determines if the bond will trade at *par*, the $100 price we spoke of earlier, at a *discount*, less than $100, or at a *premium*, which is more than $100. As I said before, bonds are often traded back and forth, bought and sold, after they are issued.

What should you consider when buying bonds? Check the *bank rate*, which is the rate at which financial institutions buy money from the government. This rate is set every Thursday afternoon at about 2:00 p.m. Eastern Standard Time. Check the *prime rate*, which is the rate banks charge their best (bigger) customers; this is the rate from which everyone works in calculating interest rates, both for lenders and borrowers. Check the long-term bond rates with your broker. And finally, think about inflation and taxation. All of these factors affect the bond market.

With bonds and debentures, you are really considering two questions: what is the quality and what is the maturity? The interest rate is determined by these two factors.
Bond departments have sophisticated computers which can help your stockbroker give you all the bond information and calculations you need. Buying and selling bonds is exciting, and you probably want to read about them in detail before you begin to buy and sell.
If you are superkeen, a book called *Inside the Yield Book*, by Sidney Homer and Martin Liebowitz, is well worth your time.

OTHER INTEREST-BEARING SECURITIES

Treasury bills

Over the last few years, Treasury bills, known affectionately as T-bills, have become the darling of everyone who seeks interest income. Treasury bills are securities issued by the federal and some provincial governments for short terms — 30-, 60-, 90-, 180-, and 360-day maturities. They offer a better rate than do savings accounts and are of higher quality since they are guaranteed by the government.

You'll see the government T-bill rate in the paper, but unfortunately you won't get it on your money. That rate is for $1,000,000 amounts. Brokerage firms can buy at these rates because they buy several million dollars worth of Treasury bills for their clients. Then they offer you a rate below the $1 million rate but above a savings account rate. The difference between the price they pay for a $1 million T-bill and what you get as your rate is their spread.

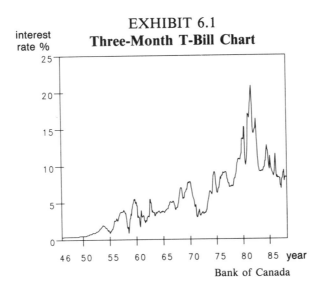

EXHIBIT 6.1
Three-Month T-Bill Chart

interest rate %

Bank of Canada

Treasury bills are issued at a discount. If you purchase a $5000 T-bill certificate with an 8¼% interest rate which matures in 180 days, you pay $4802.45 for it and it will mature at $5000.00. The $197.55 difference between your cost and the $5000 maturity is your interest payment.

Treasury bills are liquid investments, meaning they can be sold before maturity if you suddenly find you need the money. You generally can't do this with term deposits, so T-bills are a more flexible investment.

The higher rate of interest and the government guarantee have contributed to the incredible popularity of T-bills with investors like you and me.

Mortgage-backed securities
Mortgage-backed securities are one of the most recent additions to the world of interest-bearing securities. Guaranteed by Canada Mortgage and Housing Corporation (CMHC), they are sold by brokers and issued by banks and trust companies who hold mortgages, so you can have a Royal Trust or a Bank of Commerce mortgage-backed security. The issuing bank or trust company has collected a number of mortgages from their clients and put them in a pool. When you hold this security, each month you receive a blended payment composed of interest and principal, just as you would if you held the mortgage yourself.

These securities are issued in terms of about four years and generally provide you with a better rate of return than straight interest-bearing securities. They can be an alternative to setting up a mortgage to hold on your own, and you still receive a rate of interest that's better than you can get from savings accounts. And since they can be sold before their term is up, they are liquid.

Stripped coupons

What do you need to know about strips? First, you need to envision how they are created. Take a government-guaranteed bond with a $100,000 *face value* (what it is worth at maturity). Let's say this bond comes due in 20 years and the interest rate is 11%. Since interest on bonds is paid every six months, interest will be paid 40 times over the life of this bond: two times a year times 20 years. Exhibit 6.2 is a picture of what the bond looks like; notice the 40 little coupons, one to turn in for each interest payment.

EXHIBIT 6.2
A Typical Bond

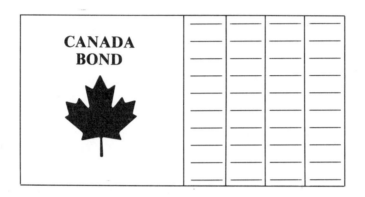

Normally you would keep this bond all together. But in Exhibit 6.3 I've taken it apart to show you what it looks like.

EXHIBIT 6.3
A Typical Bond with Coupons Stripped

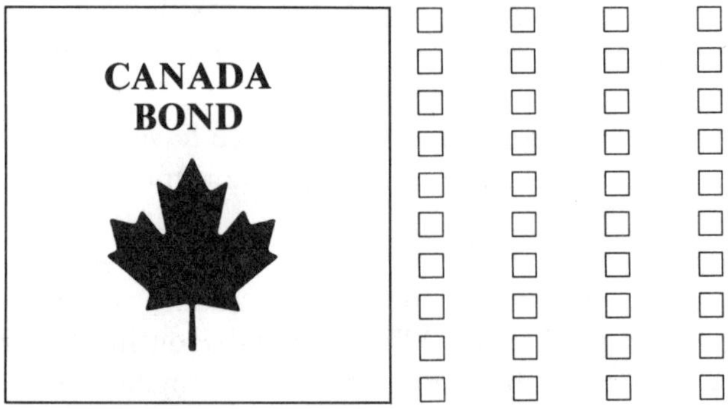

You have one big piece of paper, known as the residual, which is the bond proper. It is the part that is worth $100,000 at maturity. You also have 40 little pieces of paper, known as the — you guessed it — stripped coupons. You would have a stripped coupon (payment of interest) for April 1, 2000, of $5500 (half of 11% paid annually on a $100,000 bond), one for October 1, 2000, one for April 1, 2001, and so on. The question is, what is the stripped coupon for April 1, 2001, worth today? In other words, what is the *present value* of this interest payment which I will not receive until April 1, 2001?

Factors in determining the present value are the current prime rate, the current inflation rate, the outlook for inflation, and the long-term outlook for interest rates. Luckily for you, the bond department and the marketplace figure this out, and you get a price — say, $1547. Then (and this is done for you, too) you are given the compound annual rate of return you would receive on a $1547 investment that will mature at $5500 on April 1, 2001. The rate is about 10.23%. Now you can decide if investing in this coupon fits in with your overall investment strategy.

Today the rate (the reward) may sound good, but here are the risks:

- You have to be satisfied with the interest rate. If interest rates rise and you are in an investment with a fixed interest rate, you have lost an opportunity since by waiting you would have received a greater rate of interest. Hindsight is always 20–20.
- The coupons can be sold, but if interest rates rise, interest-bearing securities decline in price in the short term (in order to be competitive with other securities). You may have to sell them at a price lower than you paid for them, resulting in a loss.
- These coupons do not pay you a penny in income until their due date years in the future.
- The difference between $1547 and $5500 is *all interest income*. When the coupon comes due you will have $3593 in interest — which is generally taxable income — from this one investment. Therefore, the best place for this investment is in a tax-free account, such as a self-directed registered retirement savings plan (RRSP) or a registered retirement income fund (RRIF).

Obviously there are also advantages:

- You can lock in a rate that you think is good based on what you know today.
- You don't have to think about the investment again until its maturity.
- The rate of return is a *compounding* rate. Your interest rate, also known as your *yield*, is calculated as if your interest is earning interest over the life of the coupon. You do not have to worry about reinvesting.
- You buy stripped coupons at a discount to their final value payment on their due date, so you don't need to have as large a sum of money to invest.
- You know the exact dollar value your investment will have when it matures. This helps you with your planning.

Stripped coupons can also be traded. You may want to buy them with the objective of selling at a higher price before they mature. If you had purchased a $7000-interest-payment stripped coupon maturity date 2000, with a calculated yield of 12% in June 1984, you would have paid $1772.40 for it. In January 1988 this stripped coupon was worth $3797.00. It had gone up by 114% in three and a half years. Again we see the seesaw action I keep mentioning: interest rates went down during those years, so the stripped coupon went up in value.

Stripped coupons may be one of the newer products on the Banquet Table, but now there are millions of dollars worth of them in investors' accounts. They're worth your attention.

COMPOUNDING

I mentioned compounding in the previous subsection, but it deserves special attention.

A compounding return involves not only interest on your original investment, but also interest on the interest you have earned. The value of compounding is monumental. Exhibit 6.4 lists the value of a dollar earning interest which compounds annually at various rates. For example, $1.00 invested at an 8% rate of interest gives you $1.08 at the end of year one. In year two with compounding, you earn that 8% interest on $1.08, not $1.00. In other words, the interest you earned in year one is now starting to earn interest for you.

EXHIBIT 6.4
Compound Interest
($1 invested now with interest compounding annually)

Years	8.00%	9.00%	10.00%	11.00%	12.00%	13.00%	14.00%	15.00%
1	1.080	1.090	1.100	1.110	1.120	1.130	1.140	1.150
2	1.166	1.188	1.210	1.232	1.254	1.277	1.300	1.322
3	1.260	1.295	1.331	1.368	1.405	1.443	1.482	1.521
4	1.360	1.412	1.464	1.518	1.574	1.630	1.689	1.749
5	1.469	1.539	1.611	1.685	1.762	1.842	1.925	2.011
6	1.587	1.677	1.772	1.870	1.974	2.082	2.195	2.313
7	1.714	1.828	1.949	2.076	2.211	2.353	2.502	2.660
8	1.851	1.993	2.144	2.305	2.476	2.658	2.853	3.059
9	1.999	2.172	2.358	2.558	2.773	3.004	3.252	3.518
10	2.159	2.367	2.594	2.839	3.106	3.395	3.707	4.046
11	2.332	2.580	2.853	3.152	3.479	3.836	4.226	4.652
12	2.518	2.813	3.138	3.498	3.896	4.335	4.818	5.350
13	2.720	3.066	3.452	3.883	4.363	4.898	5.492	6.153
14	2.937	3.342	3.797	4.310	4.887	5.535	6.261	7.076
15	3.172	3.642	4.177	4.785	5.474	6.254	7.138	8.137
16	3.426	3.970	4.595	5.311	6.130	7.067	8.137	9.358
17	3.700	4.328	5.054	5.895	6.866	7.986	9.276	10.761
18	3.996	4.717	5.560	6.544	7.690	9.024	10.575	12.375
19	4.316	5.142	6.116	7.263	8.613	10.197	12.056	14.232
20	4.661	5.604	6.727	8.602	9.646	11.523	13.743	16.367
21	5.034	6.109	7.400	8.949	10.804	13.021	15.668	18.822
22	5.437	6.659	8.140	9.934	12.100	14.714	17.861	21.645
23	5.871	7.258	8.954	11.026	13.552	16.627	20.362	24.891
24	6.341	7.911	9.850	12.239	15.179	18.788	23.212	28.625
25	6.848	8.623	10.835	13.585	17.000	21.231	26.462	32.919
26	7.396	9.399	11.918	15.080	19.040	23.991	30.167	37.857
27	7.988	10.245	13.110	16.739	21.325	27.109	34.390	43.535
28	8.627	11.167	14.421	18.580	23.884	30.633	39.204	50.066
29	9.317	12.172	15.863	20.624	26.750	34.616	44.693	57.575
30	10.063	13.268	17.449	22.892	29.960	39.116	50.950	66.212

That chart assumes that you simply make one investment and leave it alone to compound. But suppose you keep adding money to an investment that gives you a compounding return. Let's go back to our example of $1.00 invested at 8% compounding and assume that you can add $1.00 each year at the same rate. Then you have:

End of year one: $1.00 capital put to work + ($1.00 × 8%) = $1.08
End of year two: $2.00 capital put to work + ($1.08 × 8%) + ($1.00 × 8%)
                    = $2.246
End of year three: $3.00 capital put to work + ($1.166 × 8%) + ($1.08 × 8%) +
                   ($1.00 × 8%) = $3.506

EXHIBIT 6.5
Compound Investment
($1 invested now and additional $1 invested each subsequent year,
with interest compounding annually)

Years	8.00%	9.00%	10.00%	11.00%	12.00%	13.00%	14.00%	15.00%
1	1.080	1.090	1.100	1.110	1.120	1.130	1.140	1.150
2	2.246	2.278	2.310	2.342	2.374	2.407	2.440	2.472
3	3.506	3.573	3.641	3.710	3.779	3.850	3.921	3.993
4	4.867	4.985	5.105	5.228	5.353	5.480	5.610	5.742
5	6.336	6.523	6.716	6.913	7.115	7.323	7.536	7.754
6	7.923	8.200	8.487	8.783	9.089	9.405	9.730	10.067
7	9.637	10.028	10.436	10.859	11.300	11.757	12.233	12.727
8	11.488	12.021	12.579	13.164	13.776	14.416	15.085	15.786
9	13.487	14.193	14.937	15.722	16.549	17.420	18.337	19.304
10	15.645	16.560	17.531	18.561	19.655	20.814	22.045	23.349
11	17.977	19.141	20.384	21.713	23.133	24.650	26.271	28.002
12	20.495	21.953	23.523	25.212	27.029	28.985	31.089	33.352
13	23.215	25.019	26.975	29.095	31.393	33.883	36.581	39.505
14	26.152	28.361	30.772	33.405	36.280	39.417	42.842	46.580
15	29.324	32.003	34.950	38.190	41.753	45.672	49.980	54.717
16	32.750	35.974	39.545	43.501	47.884	52.739	58.118	64.075
17	36.450	40.301	44.599	49.396	54.750	60.725	67.394	74.836
18	40.446	45.018	50.159	55.939	62.440	69.749	77.969	87.212
19	44.762	50.160	56.275	63.203	71.052	79.947	90.025	101.444
20	49.423	55.765	63.002	71.265	80.699	91.470	103.768	117.810
21	54.457	61.873	70.403	80.214	91.503	104.491	119.436	136.632
22	59.893	68.532	78.543	90.148	103.603	119.205	137.297	158.276
23	65.765	75.790	87.497	101.174	117.155	135.831	157.659	183.168
24	72.106	83.701	97.347	113.413	132.334	154.620	180.871	211.793
25	78.954	92.324	108.182	126.999	149.334	175.850	207.333	244.712
26	86.351	101.723	120.100	142.079	168.374	199.841	237.499	282.569
27	94.339	111.968	133.210	158.817	189.699	226.950	271.889	326.104
28	102.966	123.135	147.631	177.397	213.583	257.583	311.094	376.170
29	112.283	135.308	163.494	198.021	240.333	292.199	355.787	433.745
30	122.346	148.575	180.943	220.913	270.293	331.315	406.737	490.957

And so on and so on. Exhibit 6.5 shows the value of adding an additional dollar each year to the pot at various interest rates and how much that can improve your financial health.

TO EVALUATE INTEREST-BEARING CERTIFICATES
What should you be checking for when examining interest-bearing investments? First of all, know exactly what's being offered. Be careful when comparing interest rates.

A 10.75% rate for five years compounding semi-annually equals an 11% rate compounding annually.

Also, security, convenience, sales charges, liquidity, and the interest rate outlook are all to be considered. And remember my two points about quality and maturity.

When you compare advertised interest rates, you will notice that some financial institutions offer better rates than others for what appears to be the same thing. There are several possible reasons, and you need to consider them when looking at term deposits, certificates of deposit, or savings accounts.

- Some rates are compounding rates while others are non-compounding. The period of compounding — annually, semiannually, "continual" (which means daily) — also makes a difference.
- Some institutions are willing to accept a lower spread than others.
- Some interest-bearing certificates are offered by small or regional institutions that you may not be able to get to easily.
- Some institutions are less solid than others and therefore put your money at greater risk. The scandals facing failed financial institutions illustrate this risk.

Anything that seems too good to be true should be weighed extremely carefully. This is part of keeping things in perspective. When you think of the matter rationally, why would one bank or trust company offer rates so different from those offered by all the rest?

Also, consider what the difference would mean to you. Suppose one financial institution is offering a half point better yield (interest rate) — or in bond lingo, 50 basis points (100 basis points being a 1% interest rate). On a $1000 investment, this amounts to $5 per year. Driving to the outskirts of town to pick up a half point probably isn't worth the aggravation or the cost of gas.

WHEN SHOULD YOU USE INTEREST-BEARING INVESTMENTS?
When should you consider interest-bearing certificates? If you're very nervous about risk, the answer may be practically all the time. But even if you're a high flier, they may make sense in some situations.

One is when you're saving for a specific purpose, such as paying for an education or putting a down payment on a house or a car. You want a minimum amount of risk, yet you don't want to keep your money under the mattress or in a low-interest savings account.

Another good time to use short-term interest-bearing certificates is when interest rates are erratic, and you want to park your money until the dust settles. When you feel interest rates have stabilized or reached their top and you want to lock in a rate, you will probably want to choose a longer-term interest-bearing security or another type of investment.

Interest-bearing certificates have a place in many portfolios for many different reasons. With them you know your rate of return, your interest rate, and the amount that you will receive at maturity. In 99% of cases you can count on receiving the payment of interest and principal (the face value of the investment you buy) when it is promised.

The bond market is about five times as large as the stock market. That should give you an idea of how much is going on.

In this chapter we
— covered bonds and debentures, both government and corporate,
— reviewed the rating system for bonds,
— discussed Treasury bills, mortgage-backed securities, and stripped coupons,
— examined compounding,
— considered how to compare interest-bearing securities and when to use them.

Whether you participate or not, the Banquet Table offerings remain available. There are always choices. At one stage, it may be price that makes the difference as to whether you choose to participate or not. At other times the economic scenario may cause you to back away. Regardless, knowledge of your choices will make you a more intelligent investor.

Now that we have examined interest-bearing securities, we are ready to move on to stock market investments.

Chapter Seven

STOCK MARKET INVESTMENTS

You are gaining specific investment knowledge as you are reading this book. As your knowledge increases you will start to see repeating patterns in the investment world. You'll recognize more words and concepts. Your reading in the business press will become more meaningful and therefore more rewarding to you. Keep reading because the more you know, the more prepared you will be when you are ready to invest.

Now we will get into the meat and potatoes of the Banquet Table: common shares, preferred shares, and their side orders, warrants and rights.

WHY COMPANIES GO TO THE MARKET

You will recall that when a company has a great idea but lacks the money to develop the idea, one way to raise the needed cash is to go to the market and offer the public a new issue of shares. After meeting with the investment dealers (those people at an investment firm who advise them on the type of issue which might be best) and complying with the applicable securities legislation, the firm's executives issue a *preliminary prospectus*, also known as a *red herring*, to the stockbrokers. It details the company's corporate and financial plans but does not give the final details of this new issue, such as exact price or expiry dates and conversion opportunities, if any. Stockbrokers then call their clients, telling them the preliminary details of this new issue in order to determine if they are interested in buying it. This is how an issue is distributed to the investing public. After the issue is placed, a *final prospectus* with all of the details is sent to all of the purchasers. And each shareholder receives a certificate showing the number and type of shares he or she now owns (see Exhibit 7.1). These certificates can be traded.

EXHIBIT 7.1
A Typical Stock Certificate

No. 3042 — 500 SHARES

GOLD HILL MINES, LIMITED

NOT SUBJECT TO CALL — NO PERSONAL LIABILITY

AUTHORIZED CAPITAL $3,000,000. PAR VALUE OF SHARES $1.00 EACH.
HEAD OFFICE, Haileybury, Ontario
(INCORPORATED UNDER THE ONTARIO COMPANIES ACT AND SUBJECT TO PART XI THEREOF)

This is to Certify that E. T. Dunkin
is the owner of EXACTLY FIVE HUNDRED SHARES fully paid and non-assessable shares of One Dollar ($1.00) each of the Capital Stock of

GOLD HILL MINES, LIMITED
(NO PERSONAL LIABILITY)

transferable on the books of the Company by the holder hereof in person or by Attorney, duly constituted in writing on surrender of this Certificate.

This Certificate is not valid until Countersigned by the Transfer Agent and Registrar.

In Witness Whereof the said company has caused its corporate seal to be hereto affixed and this Certificate to be signed by its duly authorized officers this JUL 5 1926

Secretary. President.

COUNTERSIGNED AND REGISTERED THE ROYAL TRUST COMPANY, TORONTO. TRANSFER AGENT AND REGISTRAR. PRO MANAGER

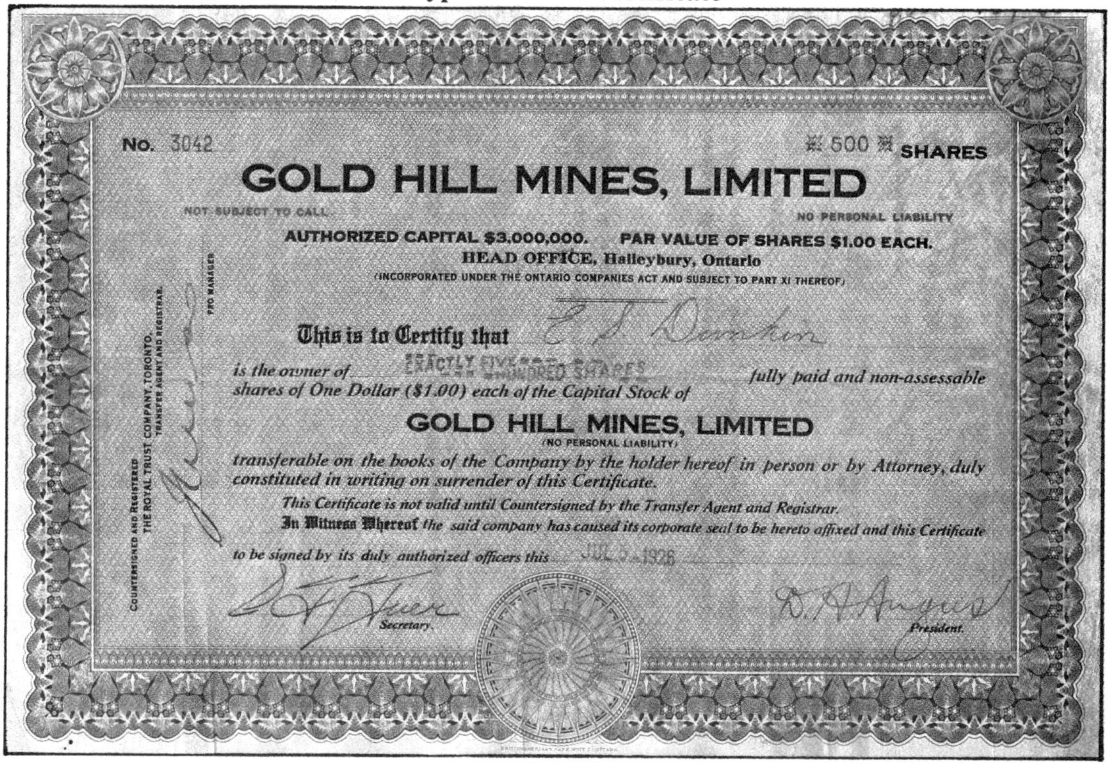

COMMON SHARES

The first shares of stock which a company offers are common shares. You put up your cash and buy these common shares. In return you get shares that can be traded publicly. A share of stock is your part ownership of a company. So far, so good.

Why buy common shares?

Growth is the number one reason you buy common shares. People want to buy these shares at one price and sell them later at a higher price. Their goal is to sell at a profit — to make a capital gain. Think back to the low-risk growth strategy and high-risk growth strategy of Chapter Four. *Growth* is the increase in price, and *capital gain* is the money you've made after you sell your securities to lock in your profit.

A secondary reason for buying common shares is to get the dividend income they may pay. *Dividends* are the money a company pays you just for being a shareholder. Often the dividend is a portion of the profits the firm has made. Sometimes a dividend is paid in shares instead of cash; this is known as a stock dividend.

Generally, when you buy common shares you are entitled to certain rights:
- a vote at shareholders' meetings, one vote for each share;
- a dividend. However, start-up and newer companies and those with financial problems (even temporary ones) tend not to pay dividends because they are using all their available cash to continue operations; and
- equal footing as a common shareholder, regardless of whether you own 11 shares or 11,000. If a dividend is paid, for example, the smallest shareholder is entitled to the same amount per share as the largest.

Non-voting shares

In addition to the regular common shares just described, some companies issue non-voting shares. One reason is that they provide a way for companies to raise money but keep control of the votes. In other cases, non-voting shares are created to allow foreign investors to invest and reap benefits of companies, such as communications firms, that the government restricts to Canadian ownership, at least in part.

What difference does a vote make? Many investors and investment counsellors will tell you that without a vote a shareholder stands on precarious ground. This is especially true in a takeover situation (one company buys — or tries to buy — another company). Business is business, and if you don't have a vote, the company trying to take over won't necessarily offer you and shareholders who have a vote the same deal for your shares. Why? Because if you don't have a vote, how will you influence any decision?

In such situations, non-voting shareholders have to convince the securities commissions or the courts that they are part-owners of the company and entitled to receive for their shares the same treatment as the holders of voting shares. In recent years, securities commissions have been extremely conscientious about cracking down on abuses of the system and protecting the rights of all shareholders. As a result, although non-voting shares are available in the marketplace, many of them carry provisions to protect their holders in case of takeovers.

In brief, if you are considering the purchase of non-voting shares, be careful and determine if they will indeed give you protection against exclusion in major corporate events.

New issue common shares
Let's look at companies that are coming to the market for the very first time. Consider these points:

- What is the history of the company? Is it already profitable but eager to expand at a faster rate? What does the balance sheet (the financial picture of the company) look like? Does the company owe a lot of people money? Why is the company trying to raise money — for expansion or to pay off debt?
- What is its product or purpose? Do you understand it? Would you buy the product yourself? What is the market for it? Are there any competitors in the field and how are they doing? Is it only a fad?
- How much risk is associated with the investment? Do you think it is an all-or-nothing proposition? Is there a chance you could lose all of your investment?

One reason that many younger companies fail is because of cash flow problems. They have more money going out than coming in. They may be on the right track and have the right idea and even the right people, but perhaps their timing is off. At any rate, they run into a cash squeeze. Is the company you are examining making sales and having cash flow into the business to pay debts and expenses? In Chapter Eleven I will recommend some books to assist you in learning more about this area of analysis. Money (cash flow) is needed to oil the company machine.

The stock of a new company cannot have a track record of trading activity in the marketplace. On the other hand, the company may have been very successful to date. Perhaps it is an old and established private company that is now going public, and you have a chance to participate in its future success. You must judge the facts, risk, and reward. But be forewarned: the new issue market can be dangerous.

When you buy a new issue you do not pay commission. But remember, you need to decide fairly quickly if you are going to buy it. I prefer that people who are first entering the market have a bit more decision time than the small amount generally available for considering new issues.

MY RECOMMENDED STRATEGY: Don't start your investment activity with new issues. You don't always have time enough to research or understand the company before you have to make the buy decision. Of course, existing listed companies may come to the market offering more common shares. That sort of new issue would be a better choice since you can know more facts about the company.

Common shares already trading on the market
If you are going to buy common shares, I recommend that you start with shares that are already trading on an exchange. This way you will have access to a track record indicating how the company has performed in the past.

If the company is large enough, some research analysts will be following it and you can get a research opinion on the stock. You can then make your decision with the benefit of a professional analyst's opinion.

There are thousands of companies with common shares available for you to purchase.

Looking at common shares on a broad basis, I come up with four categories: blue-chip stocks, emerging growth stocks, junior stocks, and penny stocks. Not all common shares are created equal. I'll show you why.

Blue-chip stocks

The term *blue-chip stock* comes from poker: on the poker table, the blue chip is usually worth the most. Blue-chip stocks are high-quality stocks, known entities in the crowded marketplace. They tend to be shares in large, established companies that have consistent earnings (net income which the company has made), make dividend payments, and display a history of profitability. These are the common stocks that generally fluctuate the least in price. Blue-chip stocks are the aristocracy of common stocks. They also tend to be the survivors. You may not get the quickest or greatest price movements up, but you won't get them on the downside either. You would consider these stocks if your objective is low-risk growth.

Growth stocks

Growth companies are those which are starting to show the features of blue-chip companies. Emerging growth stocks have had reasonably consistent earnings, and their price has gone up in the marketplace. They may not be paying dividends yet, but they have a good balance sheet (that financial picture of the company) and their prospects for the future are excellent. These shares may fall into the low-risk category, but realistically you have to consider the possibility of their being high risk.

Junior stocks

In examining junior companies, you are starting to enter the increased risk category. These shares mostly trade for less than $10, and it is unlikely that they pay a dividend. Many are the newer companies on the block, so the names are less well known. However, there can be potential here. Many resource companies fall into this category. Ultra-conservative risk-takers are not comfortable with these stocks.

Penny stocks

When you move into penny stocks — those that trade for a few cents a share — you are back to Las Vegas. When you buy anything so cheap, you know there has to be risk. Every so often the cafeteria of my university days featured something which we called mystery meat. Penny stocks are the equivalent at the financial Banquet Table. In many cases you do not know what you are getting; some penny stocks are listed and trade on stock exchanges, but many others are unlisted and trade over-the-counter (OTC). Think back to my lesson on hot tips when you think about penny stocks. They are definitely high-risk investments for high-risk investors.

Penny stocks are the stocks which tend to have wild price movements when the stock market becomes very speculative. A speculative market is really the last stage of a *bull* (rising) market, so beware — there is danger brewing.

Recently one of my colleagues told me a story. He had telephoned someone in order to offer some investment planning advice; the reply was, "I wish you had called me earlier because in 1982 I lost half a million dollars by buying penny stocks." *Beware!* I have spoken with so many people who have reasoned, "If it only costs 10 cents, then it only has to go to 20 cents for me to double my money." The simplicity of this logic is correct but misleading. For a stock trading at 10 cents to go to 20 cents appears to be a small move, but in reality it is as huge as the Grand Canyon. It doesn't happen often. Once the Toronto Stock Exchange did a survey showing the greatest price movement was with stocks trading in the $10 to $20 range.

Being a common shareholder
As a common shareholder and part owner in a company that is prospering, you may see a rise in the price of your shares and so, upon selling, reap a reward for the risk that you took when you bought them. You may also receive dividends — maybe even extra dividends if the company is doing incredibly well.

On the other hand, what if the company does not prosper? Your shares tend to fall in price, and you may not receive any dividend at all.

The blue-chip stocks are a solid cornerstone for any portfolio. If the market declines, they will go down too, but they are generally the first to rebound.

You must remember, however, that times change and the conditions that produced the blue-chip stocks sometimes change too. A blue-chip of yesterday is not necessarily a blue-chip of tomorrow. An example is Stelco, a steel company. Its common shares were blue-chip stock for many years. Then it found itself among the sunset industries, those that are contracting. It was part of an industry whose growth was in the past. Stelco's greatest challenge became how to stay alive, to change and adapt to fit the new environment for products and materials needed in the future. In February 1981, Stelco stopped paying cash dividends and began using stock for dividend payments. Until February 1982 it paid $1.80 per year, but in May 1982 the dividend was cut to $1.00.

You must keep a lookout for these types of situations because times change and so do investments. Just because your grandmother owned a stock doesn't mean that you should own it too. Watch out for companies that have become dinosaurs. Stay alert.

A piece of advice that has been proven time and time again is that when the market declines, it's a good time to buy blue-chip stocks. They are not immune to market declines, but they are the first stocks to rebound as investors' confidence returns, and they start back into the market on a blue-chip basis. You can take advantage of the circumstances, a market decline, and buy these quality companies' shares at a reduced price.

MY RECOMMENDED STRATEGY: If possible buy blue-chip stocks for your portfolio. They are the highest quality shares you can own. For moderate risk-takers, these securities are the best choice.

Growth companies also offer a reasonably good investment opportunity. You could find yourself with a winner of a company in the junior stock section, too, though you must be able to withstand the risk. But for penny stocks, be warned. I think you are absolutely on the wrong track if you use these investments in your portfolio without full and conscious awareness that all of your money is at risk.

A word of warning
Watch out for terms such as "special shares", "restricted voting shares", "non-voting

shares'', ''partly paid shares'', or any other attached adjectives to what used to be the plain vanilla common share. The company is including these descriptions for a reason. Find out what that reason is.

PREFERRED SHARES

The second issue which a company brings to market to raise capital is the preferred share. Not all companies issue preferred shares, but some companies — an example being British Columbia Telephone Company — have as many as 11 different issues of preferred shares.

On a company's balance sheet, where the financial scorecard is tallied, bonds rank first and debentures second in the sense that interest must be paid on these securities before any dividends are paid. Next in line are preferred shares. Common shares are last. Buying a preferred share gives you preferred status in the payment of dividends since these shares rank before common shares.

Like common shares, preferred shares have changed in the last few decades. In the old days, the number one reason investors bought preferred shares was to receive income. The shares cost $25 to $50, and once a quarter (every three months) they paid a fixed dividend. Shareholders would buy these shares for the dividend income, and they were rarely sold.

The fact that a preferred share's dividend is a fixed amount is important. When interest rates started rising dramatically, preferred shares became uncompetitive in the marketplace because their dividends could not be changed. So their prices had to decline to make that dividend income more competitive with interest income at contemporary rates.

This relationship between interest rates and the price of preferred shares is, by the way, typical — another example of the seesaw effect we have spoken of before. When interest rates go up, the prices of preferred shares decline in order to compete on a yield basis. A lower price for a share with a fixed dividend payment provides a higher yield. As an example, a preferred share issued at a $25 price with a $1.50 annual dividend provides a 6% dividend yield ($1.50 ÷ $25 = 6%). Now interest rates rise, requiring a dividend yield, to stay competitive, of, say, 8%. The price of the preferred share declines to $18.75, which provides an 8% dividend yield based on its fixed dividend of $1.50 ($1.50 ÷ $18.75 = 8%).

Dividends

Since in most cases you are buying preferred shares for their dividend income, it is important to know everything about the dividend and its payment. For each dividend you need to know four key pieces of information. (Your broker can give them to you.) Here is an example of how dividends are reported:

June 3   Cum dividend date
June 4   Ex dividend date
June 10   Record date
July 1   Dividend payment date

Cum is the Latin word for ''with''. The cum dividend date is the day through which you can buy the shares and still receive the next dividend. *Ex* means ''without''. The ex dividend date is the day on which purchase no longer entitles you to receive the next dividend payment. On this ex dividend date, the share price declines by the amount of the dividend, since new buyers will not receive the next payment. The record date is the day on which you must be a shareholder in order to receive the dividend. And the dividend payment date is when you are actually sent the money.

You'll remember that when you buy a stock, you are not required to pay for it for five days; this explains the difference between the cum dividend date and the record date. The payment date is several days after the record date so the company can make sure it is paying the right people and that its records are correct. These things take time to check.

Ratings of preferred shares

Like bonds, preferred shares are rated as to their creditworthiness. The highest rating is P-1, and the lowest tends to be P-4 or "unrated". These ratings are available from your stockbroker, so check out any preferred share you are considering. If you discover one that is paying a dividend quite out of line with other preferred share dividends, the rating could be the reason. As with bonds, quality determines the yield you'll be considering.

Features of preferred shares

What do preferred shares offer besides a dividend? Today's preferred shares can do everything but jump through a hoop. I'll outline some of the features. Keep in mind that these features can be used individually or in combination.

Cumulative

Cumulative dividends are a protective feature for you, more of your consumer protection plan. If the company admits financial trouble and stops paying dividends, the dividend on this type of preferred share accumulates. The company is not allowed to pay any dividend to other preferred or common shareholders until after you have been paid the accumulated back dividends.

Although this protective feature sounds good, if the company cannot pay its preferred share dividends, uncertainty has crept into the picture. If you bought the preferred share for the dividend, you're not getting your money. Nonpayment of dividends means the price of the preferred share declines. And although you may be promised first dibs on the dividend when the company starts to pay it, what happens if it never ever pays dividends again? The answer is that you won't get your back dividends regardless of this protective feature.

If the company stops paying the dividend as promised, the share will drop in price, cumulative feature or not. A $25 preferred share may drop by $5 to $10. If you believe the company can recover, you are now looking at a very interesting business risk. By buying now, you could benefit in two ways: if the company resumes payment, you will receive all of the accumulated dividends and the share price will rise (since the security is once again acting like a preferred share), providing you with a capital gain.

Cumulative shares have a safety feature, but if you have to use it, you know that the company is in trouble.

MY RECOMMENDED STRATEGY: Avoid preferred shares which do not have this feature. The company knows that it can cut dividends from non-cumulative preferred shares without having to repay them.

Redeemable or callable

The company can recall redeemable preferred shares on certain dates, paying the owners a previously specified price. (The prospectus spells out the agreed dates and prices for the company to do this.) In the past, redemption was one of the few reasons people removed preferred shares from their portfolio.

The company inserts a redemption feature to protect itself. It needs money now, but in the future it may want to clear the commitment of having to pay the fixed dividend every quarter. (Remember that so long as the shares are outstanding, it has an obligation on its books to pay dividends to preferred shareholders. If the company has cash, it could find it advantageous to buy back your shares.) People who buy preferreds with a high dividend payment when interest rates are high are sometimes shocked if the company calls the shares when the dividend rates are lower. Remember, dividend rates and interest rates go hand in hand: if one rises the other rises too.

Companies that have issued high-yielding preferred shares are most likely to want to redeem them, if they can afford it. In mid-1987, for example, Nova called its 15% cumulative redeemable preferred at $26.50. They had been issued in 1982, when rates were substantially higher than they were in 1987. Why should a company continue to pay a high dividend when it can redeem the old issue and bring a new one to market at a lower yield? If it has started to make more money, it may even have the cash to wipe this obligation off its balance sheet completely.

Just about all preferreds are priced at $25, and nowadays just about all of them have a call feature.

Straight preferred

The old-fashioned preferred shares I mentioned earlier are now often called straight preferreds. You buy the shares, and the company pays you a dividend. Few of these are issued now because investors have learned from the past and want more protective features today.

Convertible preferred

Convertible preferred shares are similar to convertible bonds or convertible debentures; the holder can exchange them for common shares at a stipulated price.

Convertible preferreds are my favourite preferreds because they combine the best features of common and preferred shares. They provide you with dividend income and the opportunity for growth. The dividend yield is not as good as you would get for a straight preferred with no extra features, but the dividend rate is a better rate than is given for the common shares. In other words, the investor sacrifices some opportunities for dividend income in order to get a chance to participate in the common share growth of the company.

Almost all convertible preferred shares are convertible into the company's common shares. The conversion ratio into common shares is generally at a 15 to 25% premium to their current price. After all, the company doesn't want to give away the store. Suppose the preferred is $25, the common shares are $10, and the conversion ratio is 15%. Here is how you calculate the conversion rate and conversion price:

$$\$10 \times 15\% = \$11.50 \text{ conversion price}$$
$$\$25 \div \$11.50 = 2.17 \text{ shares}$$

Therefore, you would be able to purchase 2.17 common shares with each of your convertible preferred shares. (Luckily, investment firms update these calculations for you monthly as prices change.)

The same calculation tells you that until the common price has risen to more than $11.50, you will not benefit from converting your preferred shares. If the common shares go up in value, they must go up by the conversion premium to make it worth considering a conversion. As the common shares rise in price, the convertible rises too because people anticipate that things are going well at the company and that bodes well for the future. Notice that this is another leveraged investment. In the example you can see that each preferred share represents 2.17 common shares. Therefore, a $1 rise in the common share price should elicit a $2.17 rise in the price of the preferred share. Most people who buy convertible preferred shares do not buy them to convert into common shares later. If the preferred shares rise in price because the common shares have risen, selling the preferred shares at a profit is generally the strategy to use. Now you have funds to purchase convertible preferred shares in another company with good potential.

Retractable
The retractable feature is the reverse of the redemption or call feature, which gives the company the right to take your shares back. The retractable feature gives you the right to require the company to take your shares back. It means that the shareholder has the right to require the company to purchase its shares at a specified price on a specified date. These details are all listed in the prospectus.

Retractable preferred shares came into vogue when investors became disillusioned with straight preferreds. When interest rates went up to record levels in the 1980s, previously issued preferred shares declined in price because of the low fixed dividend rate. If clients had to liquidate their holdings, they were in for a rude shock. As a result of this lesson, shareholders demanded more protection for their investment.

The risk here is that the company may not have the money to pay you the $25 per share it has promised. Again, keep alert for corporate developments which might indicate cash flow problems.

Floating-rate
The floating-rate feature means that the dividend payment fluctuates depending on what is happening to the prime rate (the rate banks charge their best customers).

This was another feature created for nervous (or burned) investors. It exists so that the shares should always trade at approximately the same price range they were issued in. It also means that you are not locked into a fixed dividend rate, as you are with straight preferred shares.

I am intrigued to see that Noranda, a mining company, has issued a fixed/floating-rate preferred share. ("Fixed" here means the kind of dividend I described for straight preferred shares.)

Combining features

There are a few other twists on preferred shares, but you are most likely to encounter the ones discussed above on your travels to the Banquet Table. You should know, however, that these individual features may be combined. Cominco, a mining company, offered a unit which is a deferred preferred share plus one commodity-indexed common-share-purchase warrant. It is retractable and redeemable, and there is a purchase-for-cancellation feature. You will probably notice all sorts of hybrid shares as investment firms become more creative or the clients demand more inventiveness.

If you let your stockbroker know that you are interested in preferred shares, he or she will call you with suggestions. You should know about some of these fine points because they could make a big difference in the outcome of your portfolio's performance. Familiarity with the terms is easy to acquire, and as your knowledge capital increases, you will become more confident, I promise!

Why buy preferred shares?

Preferreds are worth considering for more than just their income-generating abilities. They are also possible portfolio choices for tax reasons. The government does not regard the stock market as a giant gambling casino. Rather, it uses the tax system to encourage investors to move in the ways it prefers. You get a tax credit for receiving dividends from Canadian corporations. We'll explore this point further in Chapter Ten because it is an important reason for many Canadians' choosing to invest in preferred shares.

Preferred shares were always considered the grande dame of the world of shares, an important part of a sophisticated portfolio, because the preferred shareholders were paid dividends and ranked before common shareholders. Now the grande dame has changed with the times and undergone a revival in the minds of many investors as people of all ages consider the value of preferred shares. To compare the details of a wide variety of them, get a copy of an investment firm's preferred share report. Most firms produce one on a monthly basis, and it will provide you with all the details you'll need to know about most preferred shares, giving you a basis for comparison. There will be high-risk and low-risk preferreds for you to choose from.

Preferred and common shares make up the bulk of stock market investments, but there are also two interesting other participants: warrants and rights.

WARRANTS

Every so often a company will issue securities with a *sweetener* — an additional benefit for the purchaser, used primarily to make the new issue more attractive. The sweetener in many cases is a warrant.

A *warrant*, which can be added to a new issue of common shares, preferred shares, bonds, or debentures, is essentially a ticket allowing you to buy a certain security for a certain price within a stipulated time period. The *exercise price*, the price at which you can buy the security, is fixed for the life of the warrant. It doesn't change regardless of what the stock price does (unless the stock splits). The exercise price is almost always at a premium, say 15 to 25% above the current market price, like the convertible share premium I spoke of earlier. So if the price of the shares is $20 today and there is a 15% premium, the warrant exercise price is $23 ($20 + [$20 × 15%]). Most warrants are exercisable into common shares of a company. The new issue prospectus spells out the terms and conditions applying to the security and the warrant.

I warned you to pay attention to the redemption or call date on preferred shares. Similarly, it is critical to watch out for the expiry date on warrants. You must make an investment decision within the warrant's lifetime or else it is worth nothing. Warrants are a timed investment. Think of a clock ticking.

When the new issue is first sold, it generally trades as a unit with the warrant attached to the other security. At a time specified in the prospectus, the issuing company strips the warrant from the other security (figuratively, not physically), and now you have two trading investments. You can choose to keep one, both, or neither. Each of these investments can be traded on an exchange or on the over-the-counter market.

Why do companies issue warrants? First, to make more attractive an issue they are bringing to market. Second, to set themselves up to get more capital at a later date without having to bring out a new issue of securities and another prospectus.
(The company assumes, of course, that the price of the stock will rise over the lifetime of the warrant, so the warrants will be exercised and someone will pay the additional money to the company to get the shares.)

Trading in Warrants
What if you want to buy just the warrants? Once they are stripped from the issue, warrants are an excellent way to participate in the growth of a company if you have a limited amount of money. You can often buy warrants for one-fifth to one-third the price of the common shares. This gives you tremendous leverage, more bang for your buck.
If the stock goes up in price, the warrant goes up by a greater percentage. (Think back to our discussion of leverage and margin.) In addition, as I am sure you are saying to yourself, should the stock go down, the warrant goes down to a greater extent. You're right. Leverage, like margin, is a double-edged sword.

Your investment rationale for buying warrants is that you think the common share price will go up and hence the warrant price will go up. The warrant's trading activity is inseparable from that of the common shares.

A warrant price has two components: time value and intrinsic value. If a stock is trading below the exercise price for the warrant, then the entire value of the warrant is time value — the value of giving an investor time to make a decision. But if the stock is trading above the exercise price of the warrant, then the warrant price is composed of time value plus intrinsic (or "real") value: value that is available, should someone exercise it, that very day.

Example 1	*Example 2*
Exercise price $20	Exercise price $20
Current stock price $18	Current stock price $22
Current warrant price $3	Current warrant price $4.75
Time value $3	Time value $2.75
Intrinsic value $0	Intrinsic value $2.00

Why does the time value decline as the price rises? Generally, if a stock rises above its exercise price, then the speculative factor is diminished. Speculators frequently work on a relatively high risk parameter; for them, once the stock reaches the warrant exercise price, it has achieved its target and the warrant has less speculative appeal. It has done what the speculators thought it would, and they go on to other investments that have not yet proven themselves and therefore have greater speculative appeal. (They are just like the owners of convertible preferred shares who do not convert if the price of the preferred shares rises but, rather, sell and look for the next convertible preferred to buy.)

Also, as the warrant nears the expiry date, its time value is reduced to zero, and the warrant price may even go below its intrinsic value if the stock is trading above the exercise price. This occurs because commission costs to buy the warrants and exercise them are factored in by potential buyers. So if you own a warrant and intend to sell it, don't wait until the last moment!

Why invest in warrants?

The incredible potential for increase with warrants has caused them to be quite an interesting investment. Warrants are not just issued on those unknown companies sarcastically called Fly-by-Night Airlines. They are issued by blue-chip companies, too. Warrants offer limited risk: what you risk is whatever you paid for them, and that is less than you would have paid to buy the common shares.

Warrants also have the potential for making large increases in value. Here's an example. In late 1981 the Bank of Montreal issued preferred shares. The stock market had been declining for quite some time, so the bank issued two warrants as sweeteners to this issue. One was available immediately, and the other was issued two years later. The first warrant started trading at $6.00. Over the next few months it plunged to $1.90 as the market continued to fall. At that point the shares of Bank of Montreal were trading at $18 and the exercise price on the warrant was $29.50 until June 14, 1985, and $33.00 from then until December 15, 1988. There was no intrinsic value here.

At this point in the story, any sensible investor might ask why he or she should pay even $1.90 since the warrant was exercisable at 64% or perhaps 83% more than the current market value of the shares (a $29.50 or $33.00 exercise price versus an $18.00 current price). But within the next two years, the market improved. When the shares of the bank had risen to $33.00, the warrant was trading at $11.88. The common share price had improved 90% (not including the value of dividends), but the warrant price had increased 521%! For anyone whose objective was growth, the warrant was definitely the security to hold in this case.

I can tell you that I personally owned some of these warrants, bought at $6.00, and so did a number of my clients. As the price dropped, most of us bought more. In the end things worked out very well. Even those investors who had bought their warrants at $6.00 made almost 100% on their money. But they had to steel their nerves while the value of the warrants declined 66% to $1.90 before bottoming out and rising. Fluctuation is something you must learn to love if you are going to hold warrants.

What don't warrants offer? They do not pay any dividends. They have a limited lifetime. They can go to zero, and I have seen them do so. Your risk is your entire investment, but your reward can be a dramatic increase in value providing you with a capital gain to meet growth objectives.

If you want to trade in warrants

Many brokerages produce a warrant report, often on a quarterly basis. You pay commission to buy warrants just as you would to purchase stock. Some buyers of warrants cannot afford the price of the common shares, so they ride on the coattails of a good stock by participating in its warrants. Making the best of the current circumstances — yours and the market's — is just as applicable with warrants as it is with any other security.

What you want to be on the lookout for is a warrant representing a stock which you think has gangbuster potential. It is also comforting to have a long time until the warrant expires. Buying a warrant that has less than one year of life is treacherous. Give your investment the time to work out.

When you purchase warrants, you don't really intend to exercise them, to change them into stock by putting up the required funds. Your strategy is to buy them for growth and you want to sell them for a profit before the expiry date.

I like warrants, and I have made a lot of money on them. I use them because they provide good up-side potential and the limited down-side risk of whatever I paid for them. I once had great success creating a portfolio of warrants. I put five blue-chip companies' warrants together to make a package. It provided diversification across five different industries, and it brought *fantastic* returns. (Of course, the fact that the stock market was rising at that time did help.)

I think warrants are worth your consideration as long as you understand the risks. They can be purchased with a small portion of a moderate risk-taker's funds or with a large portion of a high risk-taker's money.

RIGHTS

Another timed investment is *rights*, which allow you to buy additional shares in a company in which you currently own shares. Like warrants, rights let you buy a specific security at a specific price within a specific time period. Rights come to you at no cost, as part of being a shareholder. For example, if you held Toronto-Dominion Bank shares in 1983, the bank informed you that all common shareholders were about to receive rights to purchase more shares. One right plus $14.625 would get you another T-D share.

Companies issue rights to save themselves time and money. Like warrants, rights are a way in which a company can raise money without always having to file a prospectus and go through the regulatory procedures. A *circular* (a shorter document explaining the details) may be all that's required. Rights allow you to buy more of what you already have, probably at a good price and without commission. If you thought it was a good idea to buy the shares in the first place, here's a chance to purchase more. Furthermore, if you want to own proportionately as much stock as you owned before the company issued the rights, you can do so only by exercising your rights. This way your proportionate share ownership in the company is not diluted (reduced) by other people's exercising their rights and buying more shares when you don't.

The exercise price — the price at which you can buy the shares with your rights — is generally just slightly below the current trading price of the shares. For example, if the shares are trading at $14.50, the offer may entitle you to buy at $14.25. The company does not attach a premium to the offer because it wants to make it attractive for you to exercise your rights and buy more shares, providing it with more money.

When the offer is announced, the shares may go up 25 or 50 cents or more. At this point the deal starts looking pretty good. Another bonus is that the offerer pays the commission to the broker; you pay only the exercise price.

Marketwise investors who decide to exercise their rights wait until the last moment to do so just in case something happens over the life of the right. For example, the market price of the shares could rise or fall dramatically because of some news.

Again like warrants, rights can also be sold. There is a bid and ask quotation — for example, $0.17 bid and $0.19 asked.

The chief difference between rights and warrants is that rights have a very short time until expiry. It may be two to three months. Rights are not used as frequently as warrants by investors, possibly because most people prefer to take more time to make up their minds. And, let's face it, there are so many more warrant choices available.

If you receive rights, good for you, you got something for nothing. It is your job now to determine how to use this windfall. The worst strategy of all in this situation is to do nothing. Either sell or exercise.

CONFLICT AND CONTRADICTION

How do you know which investments to choose? Again, you must return to your goals, your strategy, your objectives, and your temperament. Review your portfolio for asset mix: that portion of your funds you want to commit to each of cash, bonds, and stocks. What weight do you want each to have in the composition of your portfolio?

Don't be lulled into thinking that because the business press says High Flyer Aeronautic Company went up 400% last year that this was the best investment to own or that you would want it or would have chosen it. I would guess that owning this stock was an extraordinarily risky venture. Perhaps the down side, the amount you could have lost, was your total investment, and maybe you wouldn't want to assume that much risk. Perhaps it didn't fit with your strategy.

Also, your temperament is a crucial factor in your choice of investments. You want to make sure you are comfortable with your investment choices.

And be selective. Warren Buffett says in *The Money Masters*, "You buy two of everything in sight and end up with a zoo instead of a portfolio." And Philip Fisher says in the same book, "I don't want a lot of good investments; I want a few outstanding ones."

Another problem, perhaps the most difficult, to come to grips with when you are investing is contradiction. There are contradictions in this book! You need to be comfortable with the fact that not everyone has the same opinion. One newspaper will say that the experts believe that the stock market is a good place to put your money, while a magazine will tell you to avoid it completely. Then someone on television will say to put half of your money in the market. Who is right? Only time will tell. There are so many twists to the market and such a choice of investments and timing that many people can be right simultaneously or eventually.

Information becomes dated too, and minds can be changed quickly. That's why you need current facts and someone to help you interpret them.

If you tell other people about your investment decisions, some of them will tell you that you have made a good choice whereas others will probably say that you have made a big mistake. Be careful. Only you know your financial situation, goals, and level of tolerance for risk. Other people are entitled to think what they like, but they are basing their opinions on a limited amount of information about you. You must be the judge as to which investments are right for you. As I said earlier, your stockbroker will be your guide through this unknown terrain. He or she has some experience to share with you.

In this chapter we covered many things, including
- — why companies issue shares,
- — common shares,
- — features of preferred shares,
- — warrants and rights.

I have given you a lot of information in this chapter, so please refer back to it to be sure you have all of the details straight in your mind before you act.

Next, we will survey mutual funds, one of the fastest growing segments of the investment world.

Chapter Eight

MORE DELICACIES FROM THE BANQUET TABLE — MUTUAL FUNDS

At every turn of the page in this book I've stressed the importance of remembering that it's your money. Obviously you are showing an interest in your money by reading this book. I feel it is extremely important to be responsible for your money and not to blame others with regard to its handling. Sometimes it is not your fault when problems occur. But often you could have prevented them by asking the right questions. "But I don't know what to ask," I can hear you saying. Reading will help. Even a general "Is there anything I'm not looking at that I should be?" type of question is useful.

As you can see, there is a phenomenal amount of information to know about investments. At times all of the facts, figures, and charts and so many kinds of stocks, bonds, and other investments may seem overwhelming. Can you be a successful investor without having to know all the up-to-date information? Of course, with one of the greatest investment inventions of all times: mutual funds.

Mutual funds are also known as investment funds. Over the last several years they have generated a ton of publicity. The mutual fund companies are probably the best advertisers and marketers in the financial services industry.

MUTUAL FUNDS — AN EXPLANATION
Exactly what is a mutual fund? A mutual fund is an investment company which pools the dollars of its investors and, on their behalf, employs professional money managers to buy and sell a wide range of stocks, bonds, guaranteed income certificates (GICs), warrants, or other securities. These securities form the underlying portfolio of the fund. The fund has an objective, and if this objective is also *your* investment objective, you can benefit from the fund manager's expertise in buying and selling securities.

The attraction of mutual funds is that any investor can buy into them, thereby taking advantage of professional, large-scale investing tactics. In fact, for many investors, mutual funds are among the more popular offerings displayed on the Banquet Table.

When you invest in a mutual fund, you buy units or shares in the fund. You are buying into a company whose assets are a portfolio. Each unit or share that you buy represents ownership in all the fund's underlying securities, on a basis proportional to the money you have invested. So while the fund may hold two million shares in 40 different companies, your proportional ownership might be equivalent to only one share in each company in which the fund has invested.

WHY USE MUTUAL FUNDS?
The growth in popularity enjoyed by the mutual funds reflects the belief by many people that pooling their money creates advantages that an individual investor would not normally receive. From the time mutual funds were introduced in Canada in 1932, the principle has remained the same: if investors join together when putting their money into

the market, they will be able to benefit from broader diversification and reduced costs. Put another way, if big investors have certain advantages because they are big, why shouldn't smaller investors band together to become one big investor?

Currently, Canadians can invest in about 400 different mutual funds. The reason for the recent rise in popularity of mutual funds (and subsequently in the number of funds available for purchase) is that growing numbers of Canadians would like to benefit from investing but they lack the time, the large base of capital or perhaps the expertise to fulfill this desire.

A key feature of mutual funds that attracts investors is the low initial investment to get started. You can begin investing in most mutual funds for $500 to $1000. If you had $500 to invest on your own in the market, you would probably be able to buy one stock. Your success or failure would therefore depend on this one purchase. That's risky business. When you buy into a mutual fund, you are buying a portion of the total fund holdings, which may be worth many millions of dollars. The holdings of the mutual fund are diversified across the market, and your risk is therefore greatly reduced.

Mutual fund companies employ professional managers to oversee the investments. These managers make investment decisions full-time. And they make them on a discretionary basis. (This means that they do not phone you each time they make a move.) You bought the mutual fund because you had confidence that these managers would make appropriate decisions for you. You therefore expect them to stay on top of new information, new issues, and everything pertaining to the fund portfolio.

It's a fact of life — and the marketwise investor knows it — that brokers have only so much time in a day. Mutual funds are among the biggest of their big clients and therefore get a lot of attention. As an owner in a mutual fund you can effectively ride on the big-client bandwagon. It's another way of making the best use of your circumstances.

There's another reason why you may prefer to let professional managers handle your funds. They are rational about your money. It is natural that you may be somewhat emotional when it comes to your money. If you buy into a mutual fund, you are buying into the idea that the professional managers have the sophisticated expertise required to take a larger view and make profitable decisions for the fund. The concern is not what is happening to your $500; it's what's happening to the millions for which the manager is responsible. Obviously, great benefits could accrue to you from this technique.

Finally, mutual funds offer convenience. You are a busy person and simply may not have time to oversee your investments. You know what you have time to handle and what needs to be delegated to others.

Speaking personally, I love mutual funds. For the most part, I find them to be boring but beautiful. Once you have chosen your fund, you can sit back and leave the work to the experts. It may be boring not to play an active role in the specific choices, but you must know when to put your ego aside and feel confident that making this investment choice is just as important as making a specific stock selection.

PAINLESS PORTFOLIO BUILDING 2

I also love mutual funds because they are the second way in which you can employ my technique of Painless Portfolio Building.

The process of accumulating a sizeable sum of money seems impossible to many investors. With a mutual fund, $500 is a reasonable sum of money to begin with. After making this initial investment, most mutual funds offer savings plans. You can add a lump sum to your investment every so often or make regular monthly additions. My recommendation is to do it consistently every month.

You can arrange a pre-authorized monthly savings plan by signing forms which the mutual fund company has supplied to your broker. This means that you sign an authorization and cheque form which allows monthly sums to be transferred from your bank chequing account to the mutual fund company. The usual minimum monthly amount is $50 or $100 and the maximum is up to you.

Back in Chapter One we discussed the savings habit. The point here is identical: pay yourself every month, and set aside an amount for this purpose. There is no way that you could invest a monthly sum of $50 or $100 on your own — well, not profitably, anyway. With a mutual fund's monthly savings plan, you have an opportunity to invest every single month without worrying about board lots, minimum brokerage commission or anything else. Keep in mind, though, that you pay a commission on the amount of money you put into the mutual fund each month if it is a fund which charges a commission, as most of them are.

By buying units or shares regularly over a period of time, you can take advantage of *dollar-cost averaging*. This is the process whereby you don't try to pick the bottom or the top of the investment cycle. You realize that by buying when the market is up, down, and in between, you will end up with an average cost for your shares and you don't have to worry about the market's dipsy-doodling. The tortoise and hare story comes to mind here: like the tortoise, you just keep going on your course, not panicking about the daily happenings in the market.

Your monthly sum may seem like a small amount of money, but consider the coffee-maker theory. When you make coffee, the first thing that happens is one drop comes into the pot. It doesn't seem as if a cup of coffee will ever be forthcoming. But little by little, drip by drip, the water flows through; soon you have one cup, and if you keep putting water into the machine you finally have ten cups. With investing, the little bits eventually add up to a substantial investment. I have testimonials from many of my friends whom I practically *forced* to start using this Painless Portfolio Building technique. Now they thank me, but at the time it was a major struggle.

Here's an example of successful dollar-cost averaging. My friend Sheryl bought into a mutual fund for $500 in January 1985 and added $50 each month for three years. Her initial investment bought her 89.928 shares; by January 1988, she owned 362.896 shares. The prices of those shares had varied from $5.56 to $8.71 per share. That works out to an average cost lower than the January 1988 price per share of $7.14, even though she bought some of her shares at a higher price. (The reason, of course, is that some of them came at a lower price.)

For many of my friends and clients who have children, I recommend that they start a plan for their children. For a child you tend to have a longer time horizon than you do for yourself, and it can be such an easy thing to put the Family Allowance cheque (known as the baby bonus when I was growing up) into the fund each month. All those little bits of money add up to an investment which could eventually pay for your child's education or wedding or another important purpose.

At first this approach may seem boring, slow, and uneventful. That's what the hare thought about the tortoise's approach, and look what happened there! Getting rich is a boring, slow process, but it is so fulfilling when it happens. Bore me, I continue to tell people. If your goal is to be a millionaire, chances are that it won't happen the day after tomorrow, but you must get started sometime. Another proverb comes to mind: don't expect your ship to come in if you haven't set out to sea. Here's an opportunity to get started and painlessly. It doesn't cost very much to begin and maintain a consistent monthly investment plan. And it doesn't seem like such a difficult process once you have begun.

The monthly savings plan takes us back to the very important idea of exercising your investment muscle and developing good habits. Each month, when you put in that sum, the mutual fund company sends you a slip of paper called a confirmation. Compare it to the last one you received from the company, and you'll see an increase in the number of shares you own. Painless portfolio building will get you going in the right direction.

HOW DOES IT WORK?

What about the nuts and bolts of mutual fund transactions? Mutual funds are sold in thousandths of a unit or share. This means that you buy not in board lots (those standard 100-share amounts) but in specific dollar amounts. For example, $500 might buy you 39.556 shares in a fund.

When you want to find out the current value of your mutual fund shares, look in the mutual fund section of the business press, where you will find the *net asset value (NAV)*, which is sometimes called the *net asset value per share (NAVPS)*. The net asset value is the amount each unit or share in the mutual fund is worth. This is calculated by taking all of the assets in the portfolio, subtracting all the liabilities, and then dividing this amount by the total number of units or shares outstanding. Most funds are open-ended, which means that you can buy more of the same fund if you want to: it doesn't have a limit on the number of shares it can issue.

If the fund pays a dividend (you will be told if it does before you buy), you will have two options. First, you can have the mutual fund company reinvest the dividend money for you to buy more shares of the fund without charge. Or second, you can receive the dividend in cash. When you set up your mutual fund account, you indicate which option you prefer. By the way, this isn't a carved in stone decision. You can always change your mind later and switch to the other option.

If you ever need money, you can take some out of your mutual fund by cashing in part of your investment — or even all of it if you wish. Your mutual fund shares are a liquid investment. If you place a sell order, in most cases you will get your money in five business days.

Another major advantage to mutual funds is that after you have built up a sizeable holding in a fund, you can reverse the monthly savings plan process and start a monthly withdrawal plan. In this case, the mutual fund company cashes in enough shares each month to provide you with your requested amount of money and sends you a cheque.

The greatest feature of these plans is that they are extremely flexible. If you decide to increase your monthly amounts, no problem. If you decide to eliminate them for a while, no problem. They have a wonderful versatility.

TYPES OF MUTUAL FUNDS AVAILABLE

All mutual funds are not created equal. Each has a different portfolio composition, a different investment objective, and a different investment manager. In every case the mutual fund publishes a prospectus and financial statements, which clearly spell out what you need to know. The prospectus discusses why the fund was established — its investment objective, be it conservative growth or high-flying speculation — and all other relevant information. You must decide whether you want to buy into those objectives.

There are four basic types of funds available:

Equity funds

These funds are invested primarily in the stock market, and many of them have the objective of growth for their shareholders. In the portfolio you may find common shares, preferred shares, warrants, bonds, and/or cash or its equivalent (for example, Treasury bills).

Interest-bearing mutual funds, such as bond or fixed-income funds

These funds are invested in the specific interest-bearing certificates the fund is eligible to purchase. These could be bonds, Treasury bills, and/or GICs. Some mutual funds are invested in foreign securities, such as bonds from Australia or Japan.

Balanced funds

These funds combine equity and interest-bearing investments. The philosophy for the balanced fund is straightforward. Since interest-bearing securities are generally more stable in delivering a rate of return but equity funds have a better track record for growth, let's go down the middle of the road and have a fund which is essentially half and half. Balanced-fund shareholders want a better rate of return than they could get from bonds but not as much risk as they would get with a straight equity fund. They are willing to accept a lesser rate of return than equity funds can provide in return for some of the greater stability a bond fund offers.

Exotic specialty funds

These funds offer specific kinds of investments, such as just shares in oil and gas companies, in gold, in currencies, or in investments from another country. Such funds give the benefit of investing in a specific sector but with the diversity of a number of different holdings within that area. They can be particularly useful in specific situations — for example, perhaps you want to invest in a foreign country where you believe there are good investment opportunities but your access to information is limited.

PICKING A FUND

So, what's the catch? Why don't all investors use mutual funds? It may be for a variety of reasons. Perhaps they think they can do better on their own. Perhaps they think the process is too slow or the costs are too great.

As I said, not all funds are created equal. Let me highlight the factors that you must consider before purchasing units or shares in a mutual fund.

Costs: Load and no-load funds and management fees

When you are making any investment, you need to consider costs. *Load funds* are those which charge a commission when you purchase them but no commission when you sell them. The overwhelming majority of funds available are these front-end load funds.

No-load funds are those which do not charge a commission when you purchase but can have a redemption fee, which is a charge when you sell.

Both load and no-load funds have a yearly management fee. Compare the fees because they can vary dramatically.

Everyone knows, nobody does anything for nothing. I don't expect you to do your job without getting paid, and mutual fund companies employ many people who also need to be paid. The only warning I issue is that just because a fund is a no-load fund doesn't mean that it is the better fund to buy. Don't let the cost of a commission deter you from purchasing the fund. Perhaps you are paying the commission for a good reason, such as superior performance.

What can you expect in return for paying these costs to the fund of your choice? You receive quarterly reports to keep you up to date, an invitation to the annual meeting, and a year-end summary of how much you have made in interest, dividends, and capital gains. This report means that your tax reporting is made easier.

There are two time savers here: for your fees the fund managers do the investment work for you, and they report it in a simple, manageable form at year end.

Long-term investor strategy

Most of the equity and balanced mutual funds are designed for people using a long-term investment strategy for growth. If you want an investment which will pay off in less than two years, do not select one of these types of mutual funds. In this short time period, you may not make back much more than your costs.

To see why, look at this example:

Initial investment	$2000
Commission	5% of $2000 = $100
Net investment	$2000 − $100 = $1900

Your first objective must be to get back to $2000. The management fee generally adds another 1½ to 2% annually, so the way to make the return you are looking for with an equity or balanced mutual fund is to invest for the long term.

Investment goals

Once you have decided your time frame, review the priorities, goals, and strategies you set in Chapters Two and Three. Too many people are lulled into investments which do not fit their goals because of the spectacular performance figures they read in the glossy brochures. Remember your goals. Remember your risk level. Remember your time frame. Stay on course.

Track record — theory and reality

A mutual fund's track record — its past performance — is frequently used by its marketers to show how it has fared in the past. Do you remember the book *How To Lie with Statistics*? It is important to look beyond what is first presented to you. Find out if the rate of return being quoted is before or after commission and management fees. Discover if it includes reinvested dividends and if it spans both up and down market cycles. Examine all angles to make sure this investment fits your goals. Obtain a current prospectus and financial statements such as the quarterly and annual report from the funds you are considering. Read them carefully.

Evaluating track record

The Financial Times is one of the best sources of information on mutual funds. On the third Monday of every month, it issues a "Funds Survey," which is very helpful in evaluating the funds (see Exhibit 8.1).

Also, an organization called the Investment Funds Institute of Canada publishes a series of booklets on investing in mutual funds. It is located at 70 Bond Street, Toronto, Ontario M5B 1X2, or you can call (416) 363-2158.

In *The Financial Times*, funds are listed according to many categories: growth, income, RRSP eligibility, and so on. The funds are also ranked by the stability of their rates of return.

The rate of return shows the fund's track record. This tells you how each fund has performed this year and over the past few years. You can review the compound annual rate of return for one, three, five, and ten years. (Remember the incredible benefits of compounding, which we discussed in Chapter Six.) When you look at the numbers, do not stop when you find the biggest. A big return in the past does not guarantee a big return in the future. Circumstances do change. Sometimes a fund finds itself holding securities that perform well in certain markets. However, these same holdings may fare terribly when the market changes, and that will be reflected in its next performance reports.

Management changes at a fund can cause alterations to performance. The portfolio manager responsible for the past track record may be gone, so you cannot count on that person's expertise and performance. When assessing a return for a mutual fund, you should inquire whether the same managers are still place.

Many people get caught in the numbers game: they run their fingers down the page and pick the highest numbers for this year. You don't need a degree in economics to do this. But I want you to try something different — something marketwise. I am convinced that investors make big money *over the long run*. If you agree with me, don't make the typical

EXHIBIT 8.1
Funds Survey

FEBRUARY 15, 1988

FINANCIAL TIMES OF CANADA

Funds survey for periods ended January 31

43

Times variability ranking	Max sales fee %	Codes	Total assets $ mil.	% fgn	Divi-dend $	Net asset value $	Mutual Fund	1 mo.	3 mo.	1 yr.	3 yr.	5 yr.	10 yr.
N/A	9.00		3	37		20.53	Chou Associates Fund	.2	-.2	2.2			
30 4.79		LP	.45	100		37.02	Crown Life Pen Foreign Equity	1.3	2.9	-4.0	12.9	14.2	
.6 3.02	8.75		245	45		13.09	Cundill Value Fund Ltd.	.6	-.6	10.1	12.3	15.6	22.0
93 5.87		NL	.1	83		19.50	DK American Fund	-1.2	-3.4	-13.4	-9.0	-7.3	11.9
20 4.58	9.00		77	100		7.32	Dynamic American Fund	1.4	3.7	5.3	14.0	16.7	
N/A	9.00	P	20	100		4.84	Dynamic Global Fund	-5.8	-3.0	-5.8			
61 5.23			4	87		23.68	Fiducie Pret Revenu American	-2.9	-6.8	-18.9	8.7	9.7	11.8
43 5.04			13	89		14.17	Fonds Desjardins International	-1.3	-4.8	-11.7	10.8	13.3	
N/A	9.00		.1	93		5.07	G.T. Global Choice Fund.	-1.4					
N/A	9.00		.6	82		8.76	Global Strategy Americas	-1.3	-1.8	13.9			
N/A	9.00		5	75		8.13	Global Strategy Europe	-8.0	-5.9	-15.8			
N/A	9.00		20	87		9.97	Global Strategy Far East.	0.0	6.2	-4.5			
N/A	9.00		263	87		13.63	Global Strategy Fund	-2.3	1.0	-5.1			
100 8.27	8.75		13	11		5.76	Goldfund Ltd.	-12.2	-7.7	-2.9	18.5	0.8	17.0
N/A	2.00		12	100		4.99	Green Line U.S. Fund.	4.0	2.7	-4.8			
39 5.02	9.00		23	100		17.19	Guardian Growth Fund.	0.4	0.4	-7.4	3.1	4.6	13.0
89 5.80	9.00		3	100		4.42	Guardian North American Fund	5.2	4.7	-31.0	-1.1	3.0	12.8
22 4.59	9.00		27	100		.368	Guardian World Equity Fund.	-1.3	-2.1	-10.7	14.5	13.8	17.0
N/A		NL	59	44		10.01	Hume Growth & Income Fund	-0.7	-4.1	-20.5			
41 5.03	9.00		418	97		6.91	Industrial American Fund.	-0.5	4.9	-6.9	11.3	13.5	18.4
N/A	9.00		226	51		5.54	Industrial Global Fund.	-2.4	2.1	4.1			
N/A	8.50		227	83		5.08	Investors Global Fund Ltd	-4.4	-1.2	-4.3			
26 4.69	8.50		409	30		7.24	Investors Growth Fund of Cda	-2.7	-7.0	-10.3	9.1	11.6	16.0
80 5.56	8.50		201	82		9.80	Investors International Mutual	1.6	5.0	-4.1	12.1	12.0	15.0
74 5.40	8.50		185	100	.990	15.45	Investors Japanese Growth Fund.	1.1	14.3	24.7	38.9	31.2	22.8
9 3.81	8.50		288	.7	.060	7.56	Investors Mutual of Canada Ltd.	-0.7	2.8	-3.0	-6.7	10.2	13.7
78 5.54	9.00		5	100		6.56	Jones Heward American Fund	1.2	-0.1	-8.1	10.2		
56 5.19		X	709	78		15.34	MD Growth Investments Ltd.	-0.6	4.2	0.8	18.2	19.9	23.1
44 5.05	8.50		.1	97		7.73	MER Growth Fund.	-0.8	1.3	-13.4	-1.7		
N/A		NL	5	99		8.05	MONY Global Fund	-2.5	0.1				
54 5.18	9.00		40	86	0.525	14.50	Metropolitan Collective Mut	-2.0	-4.5	-23.7	-0.1	6.4	15.2
N/A	9.00		5	99		6.43	Metropolitan Speculators	-2.0	-0.6	1.3			
70 5.36	9.00		43	93	1.138	8.43	Metropolitan Venture Fund.	-1.2	-5.2	-15.0	6.1	6.6	13.7
19 4.57	9.00		7	100		13.58	Morgan Worldwide Fund.	-3.7	-6.0	-9.7	6.5		
N/A	6.00		9	92		10.25	Mutual Amerifund	2.0	7.8	-6.0			
N/A		NL	2	95		5.11	NFM U.S. Equity Fund.	.23					
81 5.57	9.00		2	97		8.90	NW Equity Fund Ltd.	-1.5	-2.9	-17.5	3.3	7.0	13.9
85 5.70			29	100	0.012	7.34	National Trust Pooled Non-Cdn.	-4.8	-0.3	-12.6	15.1	12.4	14.1
31 4.83			69	100		202.67	Natl Trust Global Fund P .	-3.9	0.5	-7.5	25.2		
63 5.28	3.00		13		0.020	6.82	Natrusco Common Share Fund	-0.9	1.3	-9.8	7.8	10.0	13.4
.0 2.29	9.00		28	32		12.04	Noram Convertible Securities	0.8	-1.6	-10.7	7.5	10.3	17.2
94 6.04	NL		27	100		20.97	PH&N Fund.	-0.3	-0.5	-10.7	-9.1	8.2	12.2
91 5.85			101	100		59.83	PH&N U.S. Pooled Pension Fund	0.3	5.9	-9.1	-8.2		
87 5.73	2.90	R	.7	100		3.86	Pacific U.S. Growth Fund.	2.9	-13.4	-2.4	0.6	6.8	
59 5.21	8.50		66	29		9.08	Provident Stock Fund Ltd.	-3.6	-1.0	-10.7	6.9	7.3	14.6
N/A	9.00		.1	86		6.54	Realgrowth Amern Trend Fund	-2.7	3.9	-0.2			
35 4.94		NL	52	100	0.024	20.20	Royal Trust A Fund	-1.2	-0.6	-7.4	11.9	10.8	12.5
N/A		NL	19	17	0.028	9.49	Royal Trust Adv Growth Fund.	-0.4	-1.7	-4.3			
N/A	9.00		8	98		19.81	Royal Trust Global Invest.	3.7	9.9	17.0			
N/A	9.00		20	100		19.81	Royal Trust J Fund.	3.7	9.9	17.0			
.4 3.01	NL		3	100		125.87	Salamander Growth	-2.2	-2.4	-0.0	9.7		
N/A		NLP	3	100		9.75	Saxon World Growth	0.6	-4.9	-5.6			
N/A		NL	1	100		9.47	Sceptre International Fund.	-4.1	-1.3	-5.2			
N/A	5.00	P	41	100		7.88	Sentinel Amer Fund	0.3	0.9				
N/A	5.00		90	100		8.26	Sentinel Global Fund	-2.5	-2.1	-14.9			
N/A			108	99		9.47	Sunset World Fund.	-2.1	1.6				
N/A	9.00		5	100		4.92	Talvest American Fund	-1.4	-0.2	-8.7			
65 5.28	9.00		25	91		4.62	Taurus Fund Ltd.	-0.9	-0.6	-21.7	-1.5	3.1	16.6
13 4.33	8.50		1273	73		16.73	Templeton Growth Fund.	1.8	1.1	-5.7	13.1	17.3	18.6
.2 2.75						72.00	Trans-Canada Shares Series B	2.6	10.3	6.7	19.4	18.5	14.1
57 5.21	9.00		523	83		9.59	Trimark Fund	2.6	2.7	-6.0	10.8	14.5	
67 5.30	1.40	P	16	100		12.87	Trust General U.S. Equity.	-4.1	-13.8	-16.0	10.8		
11 4.26	9.00		252	81		10.38	United Accumulative Fund Ltd.	2.9	2.7	-7.6	13.3	16.8	19.3
17 4.49	9.00		25	100	0.550	5.38	United American Fund Ltd.	4.7	0.2	-15.9	7.9	13.1	14.8
37 4.97	9.00		27	61		7.36	United Venture Fund Ltd.	1.8	4.8	-18.9	4.2	8.1	15.8
46 5.06	9.00		44	86		8.76	Universal Savings American	-1.0	2.9	-5.7	11.8	14.2	
N/A	9.00		47	87		4.93	Universal Savings Global Fd	-1.2	3.1	-3.6			
96 6.21	9.00		29	77		8.09	Universal Savings Pacific Fd	1.1	10.1	1.3	32.4	27.0	
N/A		R	.6	100		10.28	Walwyn International Fund	-3.1	-1.4	-7.1			
N/A		R	.4	28		8.05	Walwyn Option Equity Fund.	-0.7	5.5	-9.5			
HIGHEST IN GROUP								5.2	14.3	24.7	41.3	33.6	24.3
LOWEST IN GROUP								-12.2	-13.8	-31.0	-1.7	0.6	6.8
AVERAGE OF GROUP								-0.9	0.8	-7.0	11.3	12.3	16.0

Bond and Mortgage Funds

Times variability ranking	Max sales fee %	Codes	Total assets $ mil.	% fgn	Divi-dend $	Net asset value $	Mutual Fund	1 mo.	3 mo.	1 yr.	3 yr.	5 yr.	10 yr.
N/A		R	10		0.039	5.41	AGF Excel Cdn Bond Fund	5.9	6.7				
N/A	3.00	*	46	75	0.063	10.26	AGF Global Government Bd Fd	-4.4	4.9	12.0			
74 2.07	4.00		52		0.073	10.02	AMD Fixed Income Fd	3.8	4.3	5.2	10.8		
26 1.15	8.00		.3			3.43	All-Canadian Revenue Grwth Fnd	1.2	2.4	6.9	8.7	10.0	12.1
N/A		NL	.3			5.99	Allied Income Fund	5.1	6.2	10.9			
37 1.33			4			6.40	Altamira Income Fund	3.8	4.5	8.3	10.7	11.5	11.9
N/A	9.00		2		0.018	5.06	Bolton Tremblay Bond & Mtg	1.4		8.4			
63 1.92	9.00		6		0.050	7.79	Bullock Income Fund	3.4	3.5	2.7	7.4		
43 1.53		X	20		0.858	60.64	CDA RSP Fixed Income Fund	4.3	4.5	6.2	11.7	12.2	11.5
.7 0.61			35		0.858	92.63	Can Trust Conv Mtge Pool	0.9	2.3	9.0	11.3	12.0	12.6
96 2.56			10		0.061	9.82	Can Trust Inv Fund Income	3.4	3.7	4.8	12.3	13.4	11.5
61 1.92			184		0.062	8.57	Can Trust Pooled Income Fund.	3.4	4.1	5.2	12.0	13.6	11.2
56 1.79			179			43.43	Can Trust RRSP Mortgage Sect.	3.5	3.7	5.5	12.0	13.5	11.2
13 0.72			119			37.45	Can Trust RSP Mortgage Fund.	0.8	2.0	7.4	9.8	10.7	11.0
94 2.49	9.00		342		0.039	40.40	Canadian Trusteed Income Fund.	5.9	5.5	3.7	13.5	14.5	12.2
54 1.76	1.00	R	32		0.071	9.19	Cda Life Fixed Income S-19	4.0	4.3	4.3	11.0	12.2	10.6
46 1.66			46			8.50	Cda Cdn Convertible Debenture Fd	4.4	4.7	5.2	10.5	11.5	11.4
N/A		NL	19			5.00	Cdn Convertible Debenture Fd.	0.4	1.0	-0.9			
57 1.89	NL		8		0.061	5.00	Central Trust Mortgage Fund.	0.5	2.0	8.5	10.9	10.5	10.7
11 0.70	2.50	P	.3		0.036	5.06	Confed Dolphin Mortgage Fund	0.5	1.8	7.2	9.9	10.9	11.5
80 2.16	LP		23			322.42	Crown Life Pensions Bond Fund	5.0	5.9	5.0	7.8	9.3	8.1
28 1.16	LP		26			837.40	Crown Life Pensions Mortgage	2.2	4.0	6.2	11.4	12.9	11.3
41 1.52	5.00	P	.8		0.061	5.47	Dynamic Income Fund.	2.2	5.0	7.7	11.7	12.8	
N/A	5.00					10.21	Everest Bond Fund.	-0.1	3.8	11.7			
N/A		NLP	.1			11.47	Fds Reer St-Laurent-Obligatn	3.5	4.7	4.8			
N/A		P	1		0.039	10.63	Ficadre Obligations	3.0	3.8	5.8			
19 0.78	NL		483		0.087	11.18	First Canadian Mortgage Fund.	0.9	1.2	7.0	10.1	11.2	11.4
N/A	4.00		11		0.030	4.47	First City Income Fund	-3.3	-4.7	-6.3			
15 0.74			100		0.035	4.40	Fonds Desjardins Hypotheques.	1.1	2.6	8.2	10.4	11.2	11.4

investor mistake of falling for the flash in the pan. Successful investors are long distance runners, not sprinters.

VALUE INVESTING — THE TEMPLETON APPROACH

An example of how investing for the long run pays off is the Templeton Growth Fund. Over the past 32 years Templeton has been first in performance only three or four times. But the fund consistently produces results. Always being in the top quarter is better than being in all four quarters over time. You want your fund to perform consistently.

Sir John Templeton calls his approach Value Investing, and he has provided what he terms "28 Tips for Value Investing". I want to give you all of them so that you can benefit from the advice of a successful investor.

1. For long-term investors, there is only one objective: "maximum total real return after taxes."
2. Achieving a good record is a lot harder than most people think.
3. To avoid having all your eggs in the wrong basket at the wrong time, every investor should diversify.
4. If you buy the same securities as other people, you will have the same results as other people.
5. To buy when others are despondently selling and to sell when others are greedily buying requires the greatest fortitude and pays the greatest reward.
6. Too many investors focus on "outlook" and "trend." Therefore, more profit is made by focusing on value.
7. If a particular industry or type of security becomes popular with investors, that popularity will always prove temporary and, when lost, won't return for many years.
8. Never adopt permanently any type of asset or any selection method. Try to stay flexible, open-minded and skeptical. Long-term top results are achieved only by changing from popular to unpopular the types of securities you favor and your method of selection.
9. The fluctuation of share prices is roughly proportional to the square root of the price.
10. When any method for selecting stocks becomes popular, then switch to unpopular methods. Too many investors can spoil any share-selection method or any market-timing formula.
11. It is impossible to produce a superior performance unless you do something different from the majority.
12. In free-enterprise nations, the earnings on stock market indexes fluctuate around the replacement book value of the shares of the index.
13. The time of maximum pessimism is the best time to buy, and the time of maximum optimism is the best time to sell.
14. The time to sell an asset is when you have found a much better bargain to replace it.
15. In the stock market the only way to get a bargain is to buy what most investors are selling.
16. In the long term, the stock market indexes fluctuate around the long term upward trend of earnings per share.
17. Bear markets have always been temporary. And so have bull markets. Share prices turn upward one to twelve months before the bottom of the business cycle and vice versa.
18. The time to buy a stock is when the short-term owners have finished their selling, and the time to sell a stock is often when short-term owners have finished their buying.

19. Share prices fluctuate much more widely than values. Therefore index funds will never produce the best total return performance.
20. The skill factor in selection is largest for the common stock part of your investment.
21. An investor who has all the answers doesn't even understand the questions.
22. "This time is different" are among the most costly four words in market history.
23. Bull markets are born on pessimism, grow on skepticism, mature on optimism and die on euphoria.
24. Buying opportunities are useful only if you have money to take advantage of them.
25. If you search worldwide, you will find more bargains and better bargains than by studying only one nation. Also, you gain the safety of diversification.
26. Upward spikes do not terminate bull markets.
27. The best performance is produced by a person, not a committee.
28. If you begin with prayer, you can think more clearly and make fewer stupid mistakes.

Everyone will find something different that appeals to them in this list of 28 tips. But the words of a master investor should be heeded. His advice could save you thousands of dollars.

MY RECOMMENDED STRATEGY: With the wide variety of funds available, the chances are excellent that there is a fund that can carry out your particular strategy for you. With mutual funds, even a small investor can obtain global diversification and investment vehicle diversification. Global diversification means you can buy into a fund that invests all over the world and is therefore not restricted to one country or economy. Investment vehicle diversification means that you can get a pure bond fund, an equity fund, a money market fund, or mixtures of all of these.

One thing this means is that you have an opportunity to compile a portfolio of mutual funds to meet your needs. You might want to buy into a fixed income fund, a blue-chip equity fund, an international or global fund, a commodities fund, a real estate fund, and a currency fund. You would have yourself covered. You would be totally diversified in different investments. In a way you would have diversified your diversification.
You would own a portion of several funds and therefore a piece of hundreds of different investments. If you want protection against exposure in one area, this is the answer.

But keep in mind your costs for both purchasing and maintaining many different investment funds. Maybe one broadly diversified balanced fund is the answer to your needs, a way to help you achieve your goals with lower costs.

In summary, with mutual funds you can achieve many different investment objectives. You can have diversification, professional management, a low initial investment amount to get started, and an opportunity to add more money at regular intervals.

Mutual funds let you take advantage of the fact that the big guys get news first. Now the big guys work for you.

As a marketwise investor you realize that numbers don't mean everything. Some astute question-asking and homework are definitely required before taking the plunge.

In most cases, mutual funds fall into the reduced-risk category of investments because of their diversification. But you can lose money on mutual funds. Combine the costs, declining markets, and having to sell at an inappropriate moment, and you will lose money. But if you can stick it out for the long term with a fund, your chances of profiting are excellent on the risk and reward scale.

In the chapter we examined
    — what mutual funds can do for investors,
    — Painless Portfolio Building idea 2,
    — the fees, costs, and track records of mutual funds,
    — Templeton's 28 Tips for Value Investing.

After all this talk of putting decisions in other people's hands and playing it conservatively, let's go to the other end of the spectrum and examine exotic investments which could curl your hair with their volatility and potential for profit and loss. Put your seat belt on — this next chapter is not for the faint of heart.

Chapter Nine

EXOTIC INVESTMENTS

Now that you have a firm grounding in the more traditional or familiar investments, I'm going to introduce you to exotic investments — certain offerings that are unique or unusual. They can have a very high risk-reward ratio, and they require a specific expertise.

The investments we're going to look at are options and commodities futures. As with all the offerings described on the Banquet Table, you should understand and carefully weigh these products before you consider using them. The reason they are called exotic investments is that not very many people know about them or how to use them. To increase your "knowledge capital," you should know about these investments — what they are and what investing in them means. Although they can be dangerous, they exist for a good reason: some people want them and can use them profitably. Maybe they're not to your taste, but when the talk turns to commodities futures or options trading, you want to be familiar with the concepts. You may not want to build an atomic bomb either, but you may still want to understand the process. With this said, let's jump right into the trading pit.

OPTIONS

The theory behind options is not new: someone is willing to take on an obligation or a right and assume a risk for an opportunity in the future. Options are available on silver, bonds, and many other investments, but we shall concentrate on options on stocks.

Helpful hint: this section can be extremely confusing with a lot of terms and concepts to be understood. It requires a lot of concentration, so you need to be very alert here.

Calls and puts

Options fall into two classes, which are known as *calls* and *puts*. How does a call work? This analogy will be familiar to anyone who has ever purchased a house. When you choose a house, you put down a deposit to hold it until the closing date. If you decide not to take the house on the closing date, you forfeit your deposit and may be hauled into court. If you decide to take the house, you pay the remaining money. Call options work in somewhat the same way. If you buy a call (put a deposit down), you have the option to buy a particular stock until an expiry (closing) date for a specified price. If you choose not to take the stock, you lose the premium (deposit) you paid. The only difference between stock options and this real estate transaction is that to exercise your stock option (actually purchase the shares) you have to pay a specified additional amount for the stock. (If you put a deposit on a house, your purchase price is reduced by the amount of your deposit.)

You can buy or sell calls. In other words, you can be the owner of the house obliged to give it up for a stipulated price within a specific time frame (the call writer), or you can be the would-be purchaser (the call buyer).

It follows that if calls do one thing, puts must do the opposite. The analogy I'll use to describe puts is one from the insurance industry. If you own a property and you worry about its burning down, you buy insurance. Basically, it's back to risk and reward. The insurance company risks that there will be no fire and it can just keep your money; you risk that just in case there is a fire, you'll collect considerably more than the amount of your premium. A put works more or less the same way. You think a stock you own may decline in value. The people who sell you the put believe the stock won't go down, so they will sell you a put. This contract is for a specific stock (property) and has a specific expiry date. If your property doesn't burn down, you do not collect on your insurance. If your stock doesn't go down, you do not exercise your put option; if it does, you sell it at the pre-arranged price. Regardless of which scenario occurs, the put writer (like the insurance company) keeps the premium you paid.

And that is basically how it works. You can buy and sell puts and calls. When you do any of those things, you are making a judgement about what will happen to a specific security over a specific time. (Don't try to extend the analogies. Use them only to understand the concepts, not to make them coincide exactly.)

How investors use options

Options are contracts that allow you to trade shares of a specified stock at a particular price up until a particular date, which is never more than nine months away.

Luckily for investors, options contracts are standardized. Each option is for 100 shares (a board lot). The exercise prices are in $2.50, $5, or $10 increments, meaning you have, for example, $30, $35, and $40 exercise prices. The contracts usually expire on the third Friday of the month, with the dates usually spaced three months apart, so for a given stock three options series trade at any one time.

You may be thinking options are like warrants or rights. You are partially correct. Options are different from warrants and rights because they are more versatile, but they do share some similar features.

Earlier, when I called options exotic, I wasn't kidding. At last count there were at least 27 different investment strategies you could use with them. Even the names are mind-boggling: combinations, straddles, spreads, and so on. You can buy or sell a call, buy or sell a put, or do various combinations of buying and selling calls and puts. You can also combine options with stocks in your strategies. The possibilities are dazzling. From what I have just said, you can see the need for specific expertise when dealing in the options market. Many investors use options trading as a way of fine-tuning their portfolios. Options can also be used to reduce the volatility of a portfolio or to protect gains. You use different strategies depending on your goals and objectives.

Buying a call — What can happen

The majority of people who try options use one strategy: they buy a call. Why? Because it's pretty much the same as buying stock with the added feature of getting a bigger bang for your buck. Remember, buying a call gives you the right to buy 100 shares of a stock until a specific date at a specific price. To clarify, let's say 100 shares of the XYZ Company cost $52 per share today. The call option to buy 100 shares for the next nine months at a share price of $50 might cost $6 per share.

Who dictates that the option price should be $6? The investing public does. Like a warrant, an option's value is composed of two elements — time value and intrinsic value.

If you have the right to buy for $50 something that is trading at $52, there is $2 of intrinsic (real) value built in.

$$\text{\$6 total value} - \text{\$2 intrinsic value} = \text{\$4 time value}$$

In other words, the cost of having nine months to make a decision is $4 in this example.

Time value varies, of course, from stock to stock based on the trading activity of the particular stock and the speculative value and the excitement or volatility of the stock market in general.

To go back to the numbers in our example: excluding commission, 100 shares at $52 would cost $5200. The call option for 100 shares at $6 per share is $600 or less than 12% of the cost of buying the shares. You can begin to see why the speculator likes this type of investment. The buyer of a call has exposure to the price movements of the stock with substantially less money than it takes to buy actual shares.

What if the stock declines to $45 per share over the life of the call option contract? The call then expires and is worthless because no one will exercise a call at $50 when the market price is $45. Therefore you lose your total investment if you didn't decide to cut your losses along the way and sell the call for whatever you could get before the time value ran out. This decline in your contract price to zero happens if the stock remains anywhere below $50 on the expiry date.

In contrast if you had bought 100 actual shares at $52 that are now worth $45 per share, you have a loss "on paper" of $700. What you have going for you is that the stock could increase in value again at a later date; also you may receive a dividend from them.

But what if another scenario comes to pass? What if the share price goes up to $60? If you own the stock, it has increased $8 per share, or $800 on $5200 invested. That's about 12% (again, ignoring commission). But if you own an option allowing you to buy at $50 stock that is trading in the market at $60, that option has a $10 intrinsic value per share. If you purchased it for $600, and now sell it for at least $1000, you have a $400 profit or a 66% return on your $600 investment. As a return on invested capital, 66% is great.

Clearly, the rewards of call option trading can be substantial — if you are right. But you can see why this is a speculative venture. If you are wrong, you can lose all you invested. When buying call options, you must ask yourself the cold, hard question: are you willing to lose your total investment? With some options strategies, you can even lose more than your initial investment.

Option trading in North America
Listed options have been available in Canada since 1975. They trade here on three exchanges, and their clearing is handled through Trans Canada Options. In the United States, the main options trading floor is the Chicago Board Options Exchange, known to the industry as CBOE, which has been operating since 1973.

Not every stock has options, but options contracts are available on many large Canadian corporations, such as the Bank of Montreal, Alcan, and Northern Telecom. In the United States options are available on Eastman Kodak, IBM, and General Motors, to name some well-known examples. There are also options available on silver, bonds, foreign currencies, and gold.

Before you open an options account, the brokerage firm will send you a prospectus and have you sign an options agreement.

A twist on options trading available for the past few years is options on indexes. In this approach, you can get an option based on the behaviour of an index such as the Standard and Poors 500 which represents a basket of 500 US stocks (similar to the basket of stocks in the TSE 300 index). This type of option is known as the OEX option and is named after the symbol that the brokers must type into their quote machines in order to find the up-to-date price of the option. Instead of guessing what a particular stock will do, the investor who purchases an index option attempts to determine the trend of the market as a whole. Other options contracts — on, for example, gold stocks, or business machine stocks — are even more esoteric.

It is important to understand that in options trading the intention is usually not to exercise your options. You as an investor want to take a profit on your options, not put up more money to buy or sell stocks. Speculators intend to make money, have fun, and, they hope, stay out of trouble. Sadly, this is not always the way it turns out. One of my friends bought OEX options and lost more than $12,000 in a few weeks. You must ask yourself whether you can afford a possible loss. Again, facts, risk, and reward are always to be considered.

There are entire books devoted to options trading. If you want to explore the various strategies and more of the mysterious details of options trading, you might begin by reading one of the following books:

- Lawrence McMillan, *Options as a Strategic Investment,*
- Alexander M. Gluskin, *Confessions of an Options Strategist,*
- Any of the booklets by the Options Clearing Corporation (available from your stockbroker).

These publications describe puts, calls, and the exotica of strips, straddles, straps, naked writing, covered writing, butterfly spreads, calendar spreads, short combinations, and more. Despite these racy terms, the options market can be very conservative. These books explain the kind of conservative strategies that those who have mastered options recommend. I wish I had read them before I lost my entire options investment one year. Live and learn.

MY RECOMMENDED STRATEGY: If you are excited by the tremendous profits to be made by predicting a stock movement or the market correctly, you might consider options trading. It helps to have a mathematical mind. But please read one or all of the publications on options before you plunge in. It's simply too easy to lose all you invest. Understand the territory before you travel.

- Options commissions are greater than commissions on stocks trading. For a small investor — one with, say, one to three options contracts — the commissions could mean having to be incredibly correct before you reap any profits. Although commissions may be negotiable, there are minimums. If you want to try options trading, be sure you know what the commissions are before you place an order.

- If you decide you want to trade options, you need to find a broker who is licensed to trade them. These brokers, who must have passed a special options exam, can often be seen glued to their quote machines, scrutinizing what's happening. If you want to get into options trading, be sure you are working with a specialist, and be prepared to put in time yourself. It will require more effort on your part than if you choose to buy mutual funds or stock.

Why bother knowing about options? Options trading is often portrayed as a sexy way to make a lot of money with very little down, but don't think it doesn't have its victims. Serious options traders usually take it as a full-time task, balancing gains and losses, and they know what they are doing. Options trading is not a place for amateurs. Remember that the marketwise investor is one who knows how to size up risk and how to walk away if it appears too great. There is a warning here that most readers of this book should heed. Options trading is too risky without expert advice and the kind of staying power that only a lot of money can give.

A thorough understanding of options is obviously beyond the scope of this book, so if you are interested in this kind of investment, please read a lot more information.

FUTURES

Exciting. Romantic. Carloads of pork bellies. Beef dead or alive (listed by the foot if it's dead, and by the pound if it's alive). Gold bars. Carloads of lumber. Screams in the trading pit. That's trading commodity futures — an activity so exciting that they made a movie about it called *Trading Places*.

Step back and take a deep breath. Why did commodity futures trading come about in the first place? Originally, the idea was to protect the commodities producers and ensure supplies to the commodities users. Say a crop was due in August. Earlier that year or even the year before, the buyer and the commodity producer, the farmer, agreed on a specific price for the product and entered into a contract. The buyer would rest easy, and so would the producer. (Well, relatively easy.)

So commodity futures were set up to organize selling and buying for future use. Enter the hotshots and wheelerdealers. The speculators saw a golden opportunity to try to make a profit — by trading commodity contracts. These contracts represent large amounts of underlying commodities — two carloads of lumber, or 20 tonnes of wheat. Speculators keep an eye on the factors affecting supply and demand. Frost kills orange crops and therefore affects the price of orange juice futures. War creates uncertainty and therefore people look to precious metals and hard currencies, such as gold, for safety. Economic factors can affect whole countries. The list goes on and on. With futures more than almost any other investment, political, social, economic, and environmental factors determine success or failure.

Before your eyes light up or glaze over, contemplate this information. One commodities' manager at an investment firm told me that *87% of commodity speculators lose money*. In fact, when I mentioned this to a futures broker, he replied, "At least!" Once when I was giving a talk about futures, I asked whether any of the 40 people in the room had forayed into that market. Up went the hand of a man in his late fifties. He said that the first time he tried commodity futures, he lost $9800 in 90 minutes. Looking at the other side, someone made $9800 in 90 minutes. Let's keep this firmly in mind. You can make and you can lose a lot of money *fast* in the futures market.

Buying on margin

For the speculator, the futures market has another attraction. Most of the purchasing is done on margin, meaning that only a small amount of money is required initially.

(Go back and review the discussion of margin in Chapter Five). Of course, this approach has its risks: if you have guessed wrong, you immediately have to come up with the additional money you owe so you always maintain margin.

Let's look at an example. A futures contract of lumber is worth, say, $44,000. Your initial margin is about $4000. Margins generally range from 5 to 10% of the value of the contract. The minimum margin level is determined by the exchange where the trading activity takes place. For instance, lumber is traded on the Chicago Mercantile Exchange (CME) and gold is traded on the New York Commodity Exchange (COMEX).

You do not pay interest for the additional $40,000 needed in our example. With futures, you can use your small margin — the $4,000 — to participate in a $44,000 investment.

What happens after you buy the contract? If the contract rises in value, you can immediately withdraw your profits and still own the contract. If the contract declines in price, you are obligated to put up more money, which is known as maintenance margin.

Having to maintain the 5 to 10% margin means that you must always have extra funds available. One of the biggest risks you take here is not having staying power. Commodities can be volatile, and you may be called to cover your margin requirements in a violent downswing. If you can't come up with the money, you are sold out and can lose. Remember the figure above: 87% of speculators in commodity futures lose money. Hats off to the 13% who do make money. Until you feel pretty confident of being among those winners, maybe you'd better stay away from this volatile investment area.

Trading futures in North America
Let's say you've heard all my cautions, but you want to go ahead. Before you start, your income, net worth, and objectives will be thoroughly examined by your broker, who must be specially qualified and licensed to handle commodity futures trading. Firms that trade in commodities set minimum net worth levels, which can vary from firm to firm.
For example, some Canadian firms require investors to have at least $100,000 net worth, and some U.S. firms make it $250,000.

When you take the plunge and open a futures account, you must sign a variety of forms, some of which indicate that you understand the nature of the risk you are taking.
You indicate the type of transactions you wish to engage in. Before you sign, your licensed futures broker should explain all these risks clearly. Don't sign if you have the slightest doubt about what you are signing.

I wanted to tell you a little bit about commodity futures trading because, as with options trading, there is a great deal of hype about it. It's more glamourous to tell tales about a rollercoaster ride than to report on the smooth and unspectacular accumulation of wealth. So be it. But I can certainly understand the public amazement aroused by media coverage of the commodities market. You can understand it, you can talk about it knowledgeably, but you can also confidently say, "I've analysed the risks, and they're not for me." Period. Futures brokers have told me that they advise clients that money put into the futures market should be money that the client can afford to lose. If you can't afford it, avoid it.

Futures funds
Having said all that, I can add that one futures product could suit your investment needs if you wanted to use commodities. This is always the way it is with investments: just when

you're sure it's not right, someone comes along with a way to make it right.

To my mind, the two biggest problems associated with futures trading are that you can have unlimited liability and that you often have limited knowledge. Unlimited liability means that you can lose even more money than you have originally put in. Limited knowledge refers to the fact that people with substantial expertise and knowledge are operating in this market while you are probably just a puny little runt in the tidal wave of their trading activity. Let's face it, this is a *very* big money game.

How are you going to make an impact with your $5000? It can be like having a bow and arrow at an MX missile fight. So you must determine how to make the best of your circumstances. In the futures area you do this by joining a group of other people who think like you.

Is this beginning to sound familiar? From time to time in the futures area appear "packaged products" of futures portfolios. These are very similar to mutual funds in which investments made by the managers are in the futures market. These managers are professional futures traders who take care of the investments and make the decisions for you. Your potential losses are limited, and the returns over the long run have been spectacular.

Like mutual funds, futures funds provide a way for you to get the latest information first via your futures portfolio manager. You don't have to worry about your investment as much as if you were an individual investor because the portfolio is diversified across a number of futures contracts. For someone looking for greater rates of return via the futures market with limited risk, I feel that these types of product are far superior to trying to do it on your own. Here is a way to combat potential margin problems while still looking to benefit from the futures market. As a wise trader once said, "To last in this business you should take on a relative risk as opposed to an absolute risk."

MY RECOMMENDED STRATEGY: If you are keen to get into commodity futures, a portion of your money could be used for investments in a futures fund, as long as you are aware of the risk and reward you are facing.

As I said earlier, we are in a changing financial world, and new investment products emerge continuously. Your best stance is to be prepared by reading all you can about new investment vehicles and determine their value to you. Meanwhile, if you are interested in knowing more about futures trading, have a look at Jacob Bernstein's *Investor's Quotient*.

In this chapter we have looked at
   — options trading,
   — the commodity futures market,
   — the need for specialized knowledge when trading in these instruments,
   — the necessity of using a broker who specializes in options or futures,
   — futures funds.

Now that we have visited the wild and woolly heights of commodity futures and options, it's time to return with a thud to ground level. Let's examine tax products and tax planning.

Chapter Ten

A MARKETWISE INVESTOR'S GUIDE
TO TAX PRODUCTS AND TAX PLANNING

Throughout this book I have continually reminded you to check all angles before you invest. In particular, it is crucial to add up all the costs that will affect your rate of return on your investments.

In this chapter, we'll talk about yet another cost, your favourite and mine: taxes. If there was a hit parade of complaints in Canada, taxes would probably be close to the top. The annual April 30 deadline of accounting and paying up is one of the rituals of our national life. The bad news is that Revenue Canada is waiting at the end of the year, no matter what investments you make or don't make. The good news is that there are some important tax reasons for you to invest. You need to know about tax implications — and to plan for tax advantages — before deciding on an investment. This chapter will give you the help you need to assess tax information and products.

I have divided this chapter into two parts. First we'll take a look at tax products: investment vehicles that offer various tax benefits. In the second section we'll look at tax planning. Keep in mind that entire books are written on each of these areas (I'll refer you to some of them). Here we'll focus on the information essential for you to make continuous progress from earlier chapters with regard to investment and taxation.

TAX PRODUCTS
Tax products are sometimes called tax shelters, tax-assisted investments, or specialized investment products. All these terms amount to the same thing: an investment which gives you a break on your taxes.

Taxation is not going to go away, so you must figure out how to do the best you can with what you've got. Governments impose taxes, and governments use tax breaks to implement certain political, social, and economic policies. Tax breaks are a way for legislatures to encourage you to put your money into an area which the government wants to support. By getting you to do the supporting, the government does not have to put funds directly into the area. That's why governments can give tax breaks such as the registered home ownership savings plan and the scientific research tax credit. Remember, however, that governments can (and did, in these examples) take away tax breaks.

RRSPs
Let's get concrete using Canada's best known tax product: registered retirement savings plans (RRSPs).

RRSPs were developed to assist people in saving for their own retirement, supplementing public and private pension funds, so that the government won't have to support people when they retire. The incentive it offers is a tax break today so you can save for a happy retirement tomorrow. In 1987 Canadians had approximately $50 billion in RRSPs, and the market is still growing. These plans were first approved by Ottawa in 1957, and they have grown in popularity to the point at which just about everybody knows about them and most people use them.

The advantage of an RRSP, as you probably know, is that if you put money into one, you can use this amount (up to a specified limit) as a deduction from income on your tax form. Your tax is reduced, and maybe you even get a refund. With this kind of investment, you save tax, you save for your retirement, and the money within your plan can grow, tax free. It meets short-term and long-term needs.

Naturally, you don't completely avoid tax on the amount you contribute — you must pay it when you withdraw the money. But if you've planned carefully, by the time you make withdrawals, you will be retired and should be paying tax at a lower rate than you are now.

Within the RRSP your money grows, tax free. And if it's well invested, this growth can be further assisted by compounding. Review Chapter Six if you need a refresher on compounding. Basically, if your RRSP holds interest-bearing certificates, your money will earn interest and then the interest can earn interest, too. And it's done tax free. What a wonderful system!

Types of RRSPs
There are three basic types of registered retirement savings plans for you to consider: plans that require no management, semi-managed plans, and plans that are self-directed. Remember, even if you have an RRSP, you want to ensure that you have the right plan, one that is moving you towards your objective.

This seems the time to speak about the Canada Deposit Insurance Corporation and RRSPs. Although CDIC does not cover RRSPs, it may cover *specified investments within an RRSP.* The basic rule is that if CDIC covers an investment outside an RRSP, it covers it within one.

No-management plans
No-management RRSPs are generally interest-bearing plans. You simply go to a bank or other financial institution and inquire about its interest rates. RRSPs can offer daily interest rates or one-, three-, or five-year guaranteed investment certificates (GICs). These plans all pay you interest. You can move into one at any time, but the competitive interest rates for them are heavily advertised in the newspapers in January and February, the major buying time.

When you purchase this type of RRSP, you sign a contract with the bank or financial institution. Whichever product you select, it is important to make a note of the maturity date of your deposit. Place this note on your important planning calendar so that you remember to assess the RRSP when the security comes due and take action to reinvest the money; you may want to roll your money over into another interest-bearing certificate or you may decide to choose another type of RRSP.

It is also very important to notify the financial institution if you have a change of address. The institution will send you a notice when your deposit comes due, but every year hundreds of these notices are returned because the planholder has moved.

Reasons you may choose a no-management RRSP:
- you want extremely low risk.
- you want the convenience of not having to think about, manage, or make decisions about your plan.
- you want the promised rate of interest and the compounding of your money.
- you want the tax breaks.
- it's February 29, and you can't find any other place open.

Semi-managed plans
A semi-managed RRSP gives you a somewhat greater degree of control over your investment. Buying a semi-managed RRSP means that you buy into a mutual fund. You make that key investment decision and you have some responsibilities as the owner of this investment, but you do not make hands-on decisions. Rather, you have hired others to make the day-by-day decisions.

When considering the semi-managed option, you must read the prospectuses of the mutual funds you are considering. (See Chapter Eight if you need a quick review of mutual funds.) Only those funds with 90% of their portfolios invested in Canadian securities are eligible for RRSPs. As I pointed out earlier, the government encourages investment in areas it wishes to promote: in this case, helping investment in Canadian companies and assisting you to save for your retirement.

Mutual funds offer a wide variety of choices, so if you are interested in interest income, you might consider one with holdings in bonds. But most people who choose the semi-managed option buy a fund whose objective is growth through capital gains. Therefore the fund will be one that invests in stocks.

I describe this option as semi-managed because it is more involved than the first one. With the first option you simply go into the bank, ask for the interest rates, and make a decision. In the semi-managed case, you buy through a broker or planner, trust company, insurance agent, or bank. You should sit down with a person who is knowledgeable about funds and compare the various RRSP-eligible funds before making an investment decision. Some mutual funds are available only from specific outlets; for example, the RoyFund is available from the Royal Bank, and some offerings of insurance companies are available only from their agents. The widest variety of RRSPs are offered by brokers; they are independent fund agents, which means they do not have a vested interest in talking about specific funds.

Reasons you may choose a semi-managed plan:
- You probably want greater potential growth and are willing to take greater potential risk than the no-management planholder.
- You may wish to use the monthly savings plan (which I described in Chapter Eight as

Painless Portfolio Building 2) as a method of planning and systematically accumulating funds for your retirement.
- You may be a long-term planner, as opposed to someone nearing retirement.
- You may wish to diversify by placing some of your retirement funds in this equity vehicle.

Self-directed or self-administered plans

With a self-directed (sometimes called a self-administered) plan, you create your own RRSP. This route has the greatest flexibility and places the greatest responsibility on you. First, you must become familiar with the guidelines about which investments are eligible for the plan. Revenue Canada publishes a booklet with all the rules and regulations for RRSPs; you can obtain it simply by phoning and requesting one. (One such guideline, which I've already mentioned, is that 90% of the money must be invested in Canadian securities.) Your broker is intimately familiar with these rules.

The advantage of a self-directed plan is that you can change your mind as conditions change. If the market is jittery, you can keep your money in Treasury bills and savings investments. If the stock market looks promising, you can move to common stocks. At a later date you can switch to something else more appropriate for the situation. In other words, you have flexibility, which allows you to put into practice a cardinal rule of marketwise investment: different economic times demand different investments. But if you do not have the time and inclination for the monitoring that the self-directed route requires, then it is wiser to select someone else to stay alert for you. That means carefully choosing a mutual fund whose manager takes care of your investments.

As a caution for the self-directed route (and a way to help you size up the risks), keep this thought in mind: if you lose money in your RRSP, it's gone. You cannot put more money in to compensate and get another tax break, too. Self-directed plans also involve commission charges (when you buy and sell) and an annual administration fee.

Self-directed plans can be set up through brokers, banks, and trust companies. If you are considering this option, remember that step one is to know yourself and the good and bad features of this plan.

Before deciding on a self-directed RRSP, consider:
- How much time do you have available to spend on your investment? If the answer is none, look for an interest-bearing RRSP, probably one with GICs. If the answer is some time but limited, look for an eligible mutual fund. If the answer is more time and you have a desire to be involved, try a self-administered RRSP.
- How confident are you about making investment decisions with your RRSP? If you are not very confident yet, one of the first two options is best for the moment. If you are confident, a self-directed plan may be for you. If you are going to lie awake at nights worrying or regretting what you have done, let someone else worry for you. If you are a worrier, it's better to avoid taking the direct responsibility.
- How much money is in your RRSP? If it is less than $10,000 or $20,000 avoid a self-directed plan as the costs and lack of diversification may be prohibitive.

Rules and regulations

There is no restriction on the number of RRSPs that you can have. You are, however, restricted with regard to eligible investments and to the amount of money that you are allowed to put in annually. This annual limit is a percentage of your income up to a specified amount; it also depends on whether or not you are a member of a private pension plan. The best way to learn the most current information on this is to get the Revenue Canada booklet on RRSPs. It's updated every time there is a tax change, and it is very useful.

For more information, get out your library card again. Most public libraries have copies of the annual books that review the performance and desirability of the many RRSPs. They can provide you with a wealth of updated information on the annual crop of RRSPs and the latest rules and regulations. Two to look for: Tom Delaney's *The Delaney Report on RRSPs* and David Louis's *RRSP Strategies.*

Costs

What are the costs associated with RRSP investments? Nothing is free. When you see a newspaper ad for a "no-fee RRSP," the red flag should go up. Knowing that the company offering the RRSP is not a charitable organization, by now you should find it second nature to hunt for the fine print.

One place to start is by examining the interest rate being offered on your money. Interest-bearing RRSPs often tend to make this "no-fee" offer. It could be that the company is paying a rate of interest lower than what's available elsewhere; in other words, it is choosing to make its money on a particularly high spread. If the interest rate seems normal, check the other details. Some interest-bearing RRSPs have an annual administration fee.

For mutual fund plans, there may be a commission charge on your purchase. The commission depends on the fund that you buy. For bond mutual funds, the fee is often 1%, and for stock funds it can be as much as 9%. This fee is often negotiable or reduced when larger amounts are purchased. Remember that every mutual fund has a prospectus so you can see in black and white what you will be charged. Don't sign a contract before you read it.

Administration costs for RRSPs are typically charged annually or semi-annually. The amount may be a percentage of the assets in the plan, or it may be a flat fee — say $25. There are always minimum administration costs.

Most RRSPs also impose fees if you transfer your plan or terminate it. It is critical to know what these charges are. Only then are you in a position to determine the worth of the plan to you.

For the self-administered plan, the annual administration fee is generally in the $100 range. It is often a flat fee, rather than one based on the amount of money that you have invested in the plan. This causes some investors to wonder whether they should consolidate their money in one plan or spread it across a number of plans. The key to making this decision is to look at the advantages of each plan and then to add up the various costs of having separate plans. In addition to administration fees, there may be commission costs associated with buying and selling securities.

I know of one client who had set up seven RRSPs over the years. He found that by consolidating he saved a considerable amount of money and he reduced the paperwork required to keep track of his various plans. But that was his particular case — yours might be different.

Helpful hints to ensure that you are using your self-administered RRSP to its best advantage:

- Never fail to pay the administration fee each year. If you fail to pay it, the RRSP issuer takes the amount from your RRSP money. Pay the administrative fee with a separate cheque because it is a deductible cost of doing business. Otherwise it is $100 out of a tax-deductible plan and, therefore, not itself deductible.

- If you have chosen a self-administered RRSP and you buy securities, your purchases generally entail commissions that come out of the money in your RRSP pool. When you are investing outside an RRSP, you are able to reduce your capital gains by the commission costs; for example, if you make $2000 in capital gains but you paid $200 in commissions, your net capital gain is only $1800. Not being able to deduct these commission costs increases the base cost of your investment. If the stock costs $25, you are really paying $25 *plus* commission. Calculate this into the return you hope to earn from your self-administered plan.

Taking out money
Most RRSPs give you the flexibility *in an emergency* to collapse part of the plan early and take out money. This should be done only in cases of real emergency since it is generally unwise from a financial perspective. In whatever year you take money from your RRSP, you must pay tax on the amount withdrawn. Moreover, tax money is withheld at source, meaning that before you see your cheque, tax will be deducted. The latest figures for withholding at source (for all provinces except Quebec, where the amounts are higher) were

Amount removed	Amount withheld
Up to $5,000	10%
$5,001 to $15,000	20%
More than $15,000	30%

The government will hold onto this part of you money until you file your tax return for the year. Then you might receive a tax overpayment refund. On the other hand, you could find you owe even more tax.

An interest-bearing RRSP can be a problem for early withdrawal; if it holds a guaranteed investment certificate, you are stuck for the length of the contract — three years, five years, or whatever. With a mutual fund plan, you can take part of your money out, but remember to check the termination fee. In addition, you may be terminating your plan at an inopportune time in the stock market. Your timing could be wrong, but, as we all know, emergencies are rarely planned.

MY RECOMMENDED STRATEGY: Be aware of the risk and the growth potential of your RRSP. As you know by now, the lower the risk, the less the potential for growth of your investment. Consider your objectives. If you want your RRSP investment to grow substantially, then the mutual fund or self-administered plan is best for you. The interest-bearing funds do not have much growth potential beyond the interest rates available.

But there's another factor here: your starting position. If you are, say, five years from retirement and you want to know the exact amount that you will have for your retirement period, make sure you have a plan holding interest-bearing certificates. You can't afford a lot of risks now. If you are in your twenties or thirties, you might prefer a mutual fund or a self-administered plan so that you can invest for growth. It's early enough in your RRSP career for you to take greater chances.

Age is not a final barrier, though. The important point is that you establish your perspective, size up the risks, and then formulate your objective. Discuss all of this with your broker.

SPOUSAL PLANS

I'm often asked what should happen if you make lots of money and your spouse makes less or nothing. You can establish a spousal plan, which means your making an eligible contribution in the name of your spouse. Most people do this because they anticipate that when the RRSP money is withdrawn, the spouse will be in a lower tax bracket and therefore will pay less tax. Your advantage comes in the form of a tax savings now because you receive the greatest benefit as the highest taxpayer from the deduction today.

Keep in mind that the amount you contribute to the spousal plan must fall within your personal limit. A spouse who has earned income can also contribute independently to his or her own plan.

WHAT HAPPENS AFTER RRSPS? — RRIFS

The law requires you to collapse your RRSP when you reach age 71, but there is an alternative. It's the graduate RRSP, known as a registered retirement income fund (RRIF for short). If you do not want to take your money out of your RRSP in a lump or buy an annuity, the RRIF allows you to continue deferring tax while your investment continues to grow. When you buy an annuity, it offers you a fixed monthly payment, whereas an RRIF offers you flexibility and control over the investments within the plan. Many people who have had self-administered RRSPs just carry on the process by having a self-administered RRIF. There are also mutual fund RRIFs.

Revenue Canada offers a pamphlet with the guidelines for RRIFs. Your RRIF can continue to generate income. Each year you are required to take out a certain amount of money (stated in the guidelines), and you must withdraw all of your funds by age 90. As each sum is withdrawn, you pay tax on the withdrawn amount. This type of graduate RRSP is an excellent choice for people who want to maintain control over the investments that their retirement funds have purchased. In 1986 the rules on RRIFs were dramatically altered to increase their flexibility. Now you have much greater control over your funds, which is why this alternative deserves special consideration.

I like RRIFs far better than annuities because they provide greater flexibility and they do not restrict the withdrawal of funds, should you need or want them. You can also own both an annuity and an RRIF, or you can buy one and, if you change your mind at a later date, switch into the other choice. There are costs for switching and so on, so you need to examine all the information before making a choice.

REAL ESTATE PARTNERSHIPS

As already discussed, the government gives tax breaks to stimulate investment in certain areas. Some real estate projects are set up as partnerships, and for the purposes of the tax department are eligible for certain tax breaks. The company behind the development is looking for a way to reduce the tremendous risk and cost of real estate development, so they look for investors to share the risk.

A real estate partnership you can buy into is offered in units, and a prospectus is always issued. Your broker is a good source of information if this type of investment appeals to you. The unit prices can vary from $5,000 up to $150,000 for real estate partnerships. These, like all tax-driven investments, are good to consider if you are in the top tax brackets. Below this level, check closely to see if you will benefit.

MY RECOMMENDED STRATEGY: Don't ever buy an investment just because it is a tax shelter. It must first stand on its own merits as an investment.

Remember always to check the latest government legislation with regard to any tax product. It may be affected by various tax rules and regulations, many of which are changed frequently.

WILD AND WOOLLY TAX SHELTERS: BE PREPARED FOR THE RIDE

Just as government can decide to create a tax shelter, it can also decide to take one away. Sometimes the government changes its mind because it believes the tax stimulation is no longer needed. Sometimes it feels that there have been abuses of a tax shelter. Minister of Finance Michael Wilson once referred to this kind of action as "the marrying of two different sections of the tax act which were never intended to be put together."
Enter what I refer to as the wild and woolly tax shelters.

Over the years there have been tax shelters based on products as diverse as yachts, race horses, and movies. Not long ago there was the widely publicized Scientific Research Tax Credit. It certainly made sense for the government to encourage research and development, but abuses were detected in the use of SRTCs. The fakes were closed down — along with some legitimate products — and the tax shelter was ended. The government knows there is a big difference between tax evasion and tax reduction.

Only foolhardy investors put money in a product solely for the tax write-off. But every year many tax-shelter products show up in December. The issuers know that people are desperate. They feel that they have to have a tax shelter by December 31, so they tend to be less choosy. It's important to know what the product is, to learn who is running the company and what their success has been so far, and to gain a sense of the direction in which the company is headed.

Again, the practical advice is don't invest in something simply because it is a tax shelter. It's dangerous to play around with wild tax products. If the government figures out that foul play has occurred, you run the risk of fines and having the tax deduction disallowed.

When considering a tax product, be it ordinary or out of the ordinary, examine it carefully. Ask these few questions before you make a move.

- In the best case, what's my highest potential return, in addition to the tax savings that could result?
- How long must I keep my money in this investment before I see the result?
- Is the investment liquid — can I sell and get out?
- Can I sell the investment without restrictions? how easily?
- What is the worst possible outcome, the biggest downside? If someone says there is no downside, shake hands and say good-bye. Be realistic. It's hard to imagine a tax-driven investment without some downside.
- How much time will it take me as an investor to administer this investment?
- What will the reporting system be? How often will I be kept informed?
- How complicated will the tax reporting be?
- Is there any requirement that investors will or may be called on to put up additional funds?

It can be a good idea to gain perspective by seeking independent advice. Many tax advisors will have worked with similar tax products before. They cannot tell you whether or not this will be a good investment, but they can say how this deal compares to others they've seen. Brokers can tell you the track record of the people involved (since many tax shelters are repeated each year by the same company) and the investment climate for the tax product you are considering. Remember that brokers cannot give you tax advice, only tax information. Lawyers and accountants are better equipped to give tax advice. Many brokers have, however, become quite knowledgeable in the tax product field and can give you the solid information you need to consider before buying this product.

Finally, caveat emptor ("buyer beware") on these deals. Don't let the tax advantages cloud your vision. Always keep in mind that while the product may be a good tax product, in the end the proof of its value will be whether or not it is also a good investment.

TAX PLANNING

Before we begin this section, I want you to take a moment to review how far you have come, how much progress you have made towards your goal of understanding investments and making informed decisions about your money. In the first three chapters, "Get Ready", "Get Set", and "Go For It", you set up a system and looked at your starting point. Then after an introduction to brokers, the stock market, and the Banquet Table of potential investments, we worked our way through some of the major marketplace offerings. Now you know what is out there. You have indeed come a long way.

We shall continue in this section to develop strategies and plans. Now you are familiar with the offerings, you should be thinking about how to take maximum advantage of all these products, from common stocks to warrants, bonds, and tax products. Above all, an investor is a planner. Here we'll focus specifically on planning your financial future.

It has always intrigued me that in mid December, as sure as there is a Christmas, I will receive calls from people seeking tax help — not for the next tax year, which would make sense, but for the current year that is rapidly coming to an end. But if you leave tax planning until the end of the year, there's little that can be done other than to make the maximum contribution to the best RRSP you can find. Planning is about anticipating and organizing an approach before you actually face the situation, not about facing it after it is 99% through. You want to avoid planning when your time is nearly up.

Here are my observations on what you should take into account when you do your very important planning.

Planning Idea 1 — RRSPs

Is an RRSP the best place for you to put your money? Perhaps. It is the most popular investment for Canadians, but should you be among them?

For example, you have to determine if you are using this tax product for the tax deduction or to save for your retirement. If you are in a low income bracket, and therefore not obligated to pay much tax, the tax saving may not be that beneficial. And an RRSP may not be the best way for you to plan for your retirement. You might be better off starting a mutual fund. In that case, your goal would be capital gains. There would be no special tax break today, as you would get for the RRSP, but at your tax level this may not be very important. Your goal is the long-term one of saving money for your retirement.

Another better plan for the long run may be paying down your mortgage. By doing this your house becomes your retirement asset. You should compare the interest you'll pay on your mortgage versus the rate of return your RRSP would provide.

When you consider an RRSP (and judging by their popularity, most people have), you discover that about 400 plans are available in Canada. Most people look into the possibilities in January and February — the 60 days after year end when you can put money into an RRSP and reduce your previous year's earned income. This, of course, is the wrong time to be considering an RRSP; everyone who sells them is so stressed out by then that they can barely speak. My advice is to plan ahead. Determine your RRSP investment by talking to people in late March, when everyone has had a chance to recover yet still has all the rules and regulations fresh in mind.

Here's another point to consider: the time to start retirement saving is *now*. The age at which you retire will vary based on factors beyond the scope of this book. Whenever it happens, I'm sure you'd agree that retirement with $1 million would be good. (It would be even better if you had it today, but alas everyone can't win the lottery.) Take a look at Exhibit 10.1 to see why starting retirement saving early is such a good idea. Do this for yourself if you can, or suggest it to your children if they are at this age.

Saving Susan put $5500 into an RRSP at age 25 and in every year thereafter until she reached age 31. Then Susan stopped adding money. It's a conservative RRSP with interest earned at the rate of 10% per year compounded annually. When Susan reaches age 61, there it is: $1 million in her plan. The secret is compounding. Starting early is the key. If you can, start as early as possible. But if you didn't start early, it is better to start late than not to start at all. Of course, if Susan keeps adding money each year, she'll continue to receive a tax saving and defer tax on her interest until retirement when she'll be even richer than a millionaire.

EXHIBIT 10.1
Saving Susan's RRSP

Assume the money is put in on January 1, with interest compounding at 10% annually.

Age	Money Contributed	Interest	Value at Year-End
25	5500	10%	$ 6050
26	5500	10	12,705
27	5500	10	20,025
28	5500	10	28,078
29	5500	10	36,936
30	5500	10	46,679
31	5500	10	57,397
35	0	10	84,030
40	0	10	135,372
45	0	10	218,084
50	0	10	351,334
55	0	10	565,999
60	0	10	911,824
61	0	10	1,003,006

If Susan waits until age 65 to retire, she will have $1,468,410. If she waits until age 71, she will have $2,602,006.

P.S. If Susan keeps contributing $5500 annually to her RRSP from age 25, she will reach the $1 million mark at the end of the year in which she turns 55: six years earlier than in the example shown. These examples illustrate the value of compounding and how the numbers go wild in the later years.

The point here as with all investing is not to buy into the prevailing wisdom without taking a hard look at your own situation. Plan over the long term for how *you* can make the most of what *you've* got. This book is not designed to be tax-comprehensive. (I've suggested in discussing RRSPs and in other sections that you consult other sources of information for further details on some of these investment products.) What I do hope to do is to prime you so that you know that you have to stay alert and keep on top of changes that may affect your planning.

Also, put your RRSP money in early, and you'll increase your RRSP simply because the money will be compounding longer. Revenue Canada allows you 60 days after the end of the calendar year to make an RRSP contribution, but don't wait that long. You want to put your money into your plan months before, to get it working for you as quickly as possible.

Planning Idea 2 — Your capital gains exemption

In 1985, Finance Minister Michael Wilson made history for investors when he announced a $500,000 lifetime capital gains exemption. Later he rewrote history by proposing to change that limit to $100,000.

Under the system in force from 1972 to 1985, an investor was taxed on half the capital gains he or she made. If you bought a stock at $5 and sold it at $10, the capital gain is $5. Investors were taxed at their marginal tax rate on half the gain, or $2.50 of a $5 capital gain.

Under the proposed new system, you would be allowed to make $100,000 in capital gains tax free in your lifetime and then be taxed on any capital gains beyond this amount.

The current proposals state that in 1988 two-thirds of those non-exempt capital gains would be taxed. In our example above, supposing that you'd used up or were holding for later your lifetime exemption, $3.33 of the $5 gain would be taxable. In 1990 this amount would increase to 75%, or $3.75 of the $5 gain. As with all government plans, there are certain to be refinements.

There are specific criteria regarding capital gains taxation and the lifetime exemption, so check to make sure you have up-to-date data. It is wise to check about any investment before putting your money down or selling anything. Check with Revenue Canada, a tax expert, or your brokerage firm, and monitor the business press for the latest developments on taxation and investment.

At the moment, this $100,000 exemption is a great opportunity. Cottages, Canadian stocks, US stocks, even baseball cards are all eligible so far. Use this important tax advantage.

It is your responsibility to report capital gains in the year in which they occur. In order to achieve a capital gain in a particular taxation year, remember to contact your broker well before the last day of the month. The reason is that the sell transaction must be done five business days before the end of December to count for that tax year. For planning purposes, mark December 1 on your calendar as the date to sort out your final plans.

Planning Idea 3 — Dividend and interest income

The dividends you receive from Canadian corporations are eligible for the dividend gross-up and tax credit, a method the government provides to give you a tax break on dividend income. So you should calculate the after-tax result of receiving dividends in order to compare dividend and interest income fairly.

Suppose you receive a $100 dividend. Here is how the gross-up and tax credit work. (For this example, we'll calculate the federal tax at 29%; which is the rate for those in the top bracket, and we'll assume a provincial tax of 50% of the net federal tax and ignore surtaxes.)

Cash dividend	$100.00
25% gross-up	+ 25.00
Taxable dividend	$125.00
Unadjusted federal tax	$ 36.25
Dividend tax credit	− 16.67
Net federal tax	$ 19.58
Provincial tax	+ 9.79
Combined tax	$29.37.

This leaves you with a net after-tax amount of $70.63 for each $100 you receive in dividends.

How does this after-tax return compare to what you receive on interest income? Interest is subject to tax without any benefits. Why is the tax structure the way it is, you may ask. The whole question may be unanswerable, but on the point of interest income it's pretty simple. The government knows what you know: that minimal risk is associated with earning interest income. If your money is in a financial institution, the Canada Deposit Insurance Corporation protects up to $60,000 of your savings. Where there is little risk, the government enforces full taxation. No risk, no tax breaks seems to be the way it thinks.

Back to our comparison of dividend and interest income. Someone in the top tax bracket is charged approximately 45% (combined federal and provincial tax) on any interest income. Therefore, $100 in interest income results in $55 after-tax income.

Completing complicated calculations when you are comparing dividends and interest income is too much to ask anyone. But there's a good general rule of thumb:

An interest payment of $1.27 approximately equals $1.00 of dividend income.

To put this another way, you can multiply your dividend yield (remember, the ratio calculated by dividing your dividend by the cost of your stock) by 1.27%.

If you had an 8% dividend yield, what rate of interest would you need to equal this dividend *after-taxes*?

$$8\% \times 1.27 = 10.16\%$$

Therefore, you need to obtain a 10.16% interest rate to roughly approximate an 8% dividend yield.

Here are the comparable figures for dividend and interest income for all tax brackets:

Taxable income	After-tax interest kept	After-tax dividends kept
Less than $27,500	$74.50	$93.13
$27,501 to $55,000	$61.00	$76.25
More than $55,000	$56.50	$70.63

For your tax reporting, one of the benefits of dealing with financial institutions is that they send you T-5 slips stating your dividend and interest income. The same is true of mutual funds, which provide a breakdown of dividend and interest income and capital gains. If you keep your stock certificates with a brokerage firm, it will also send you T-5 slips detailing dividend and interest income. If you hold your stock certificates yourself, your dividend comes directly from the company, and you can expect to receive a T-5 directly.

You should keep all this information together in your A-Z file. It is a crime in Canada not to report income. You are obliged to prove what you say, so keep those slips of paper.

Planning Idea 4 — Tax products
If you are contemplating the purchase of a tax product, try to avoid buying in December. There's a mad frenzy at that time. If you know that you will require a tax product, take a leisurely look at them over the year. Remember that you are looking for investment merits first and tax implications second. This can be done much more efficiently at a time when you are not pressured. If you desperately need to reduce your tax burden at year end, you are ripe for a potentially regrettable investment decision. Be prepared.

Planning Idea 5 — Double checking
Many people prepare their own tax returns. You may want to have a tax advisor review your return before you send it in. This is a useful exercise because there may be something you have overlooked. A review does not cost you as much as a full preparation since you have done the preparation work yourself.

Eventually, if your return becomes more complicated, it is worth the money to hire a tax-preparation specialist. However, your money is still yours. Don't lose touch with the details of your financial status and current tax situation just because you are paying someone else to take care of it for you.

Planning Idea 6 — When to get professional advice
A number of tax-deductible items are associated with investing. You probably know about some, such as the fact that interest you pay on money borrowed for purposes of investment is a tax-deductible expense (within certain guidelines).

At some point, you will find it worthwhile to see a professional tax advisor. Go prepared, so that you can use the time most efficiently. You want to be in a position to present clearly and quickly the highlights of your tax situation, accompanied by a copy of your return. You want to outline the ways in which you are taking advantage of any deductions available to you and any thoughts you may have on your future tax position and investment options. Some fees for seeking this advice are a deductible expense, but ask first before assuming.

Then you want to listen and ask questions to be sure you understand. The professional you select spends most of his or her time considering the day-in, day-out details of tax returns. You want to have the benefit of this experience applied to your tax case.
You may hear some insightful information allowing you to improve your tax savings.
You may learn about new avenues which could benefit you substantially over the longer

term. Or, just as helpful, you may hear that you are on the right track and have the situation basically in hand. The point is that it pays to have an expert confirm the correctness of your strategies.

How do you find an advisor? Start by asking your close associates for their recommendations. The advantage here is that you are likely to be given the name of someone who has already proven his or her worth to your associate over the years. If your associate is in the same business you are, the recommended advisor is probably familiar with your industry. Taxation is such a complex field that there may be advantages in finding someone who has some specialization in the type of information on your tax return. Many tax specialists are generalists, but a tax expert who is experienced at handling the ins and outs of returns containing your type of information may take less time to size up your situation and to make concrete recommendations. This could save you time and money.

Your broker is another potential source of suggestions about tax advisors. He or she has worked with numerous professionals and can refer you to someone appropriate.

If you prefer, call one of the accounting firms. They all have people who specialize in taxes. Tell them your annual income and ask whether they handle people like you. On the subject of questions, *before* you go to a meeting with a potential advisor, ask how much it will cost. You will generally be quoted an hourly rate. This will provide you with an incentive to have as comprehensive a picture as possible ready to show the tax advisor at your meeting.

Before you go to see this person, I recommend that you read one of the many books available on taxes. One of my favourites is David Louis' book *Tax-Saving Strategies for the Canadian Investor*. It is important to keep up with changes that may affect you, so why not spend a few hours reading? In the library you can find all the latest tax guides useful to people such as yourself.

You might want to concentrate on the sections of these tax books that tell you what's new from Revenue Canada. It is always in your interest to check the actual Revenue Canada bulletins to confirm the details of the benefits you want to claim. If you can't find what you need in your library, phone or write the closest Revenue Canada office.

Many people who might not otherwise be investors get into the market because they want to defer tax. If you are among this group, make sure that you keep reading about tax products to keep up to date. RRSPs are only the beginning, as you have seen in this chapter!

Planning Idea 7 — Co-ordinating your advisors
As I have said before, brokers are not allowed to give tax advice. They can give you important tax information, and they can tell you in general about the tax implications of some of your investment decisions. But don't be misled into thinking that theirs is the last word on the subject. Your situation could have a particular twist to it that the broker does not know. It is probably worth your while to get specific tax advice. This will allow you to review your total financial position and see how this investment will affect your tax position.

Taking this action calls for co-ordination. Suppose you have received information about a tax product such as a real estate partnership. You may wish to go to a tax advisor who can say whether the tax benefit would apply to you, whether it is in your interests to consider this investment, and possibly whether this is the best route for you to go to achieve the tax position you want.

You also want to talk to your broker — and possibly your lawyer — about the details of the product and how it fits your goals. When you're talking to one advisor, tell him or her what the other said, or put them in touch with each other.

Listen to your advisors. Then reach a conclusion that is right for *you*. More and more tax advisors are realizing the incredible complexity of some products and aiming to co-ordinate their tax knowledge with the investment knowledge of the broker. It is not a competition to see who will win. You must win. Tax advisors want to keep you out of trouble, and their job is to comment on your total financial picture as well as on the tax implications of a particular investment.

Look at the facts that can help you to make a decision that is in your best all-round interest. By looking at the tax implications before you devise your investment strategy and by continually reviewing your position, you can make the most of what you have.
And that's marketwise!

In this chapter we have covered
   — RRSPs, and the pros and cons of the available plans,
   — RRIFs,
   — real estate partnerships and other tax shelters,
   — dividend versus interest income,
   — seven planning ideas.

Get ready now to take a look at some sources of information you may want to use and understand as an investor.

Chapter Eleven

HOW TO GATHER INVESTMENT INFORMATION, READ BETWEEN THE LINES, AND DECODE JARGON

At the beginning of this book I mentioned that there is no shortage of information in the investment industry. Rather, the problem is that there is so *much* information.
The industry is peopled with great talkers and prolific writers. You could easily be overwhelmed by all this data, but you won't be once you learn a few simple techniques for filtering information. It's worth spending a bit of time now absorbing these techniques because it will save you a lot of time later as you read more. And your time is valuable.

One of the things we constantly face in the investment industry is cyclicality. "Cyclicality" is the word used to describe how things that happened in the past have a funny way of happening again. It is for this reason that I recommend you listen to what the knowledgeable veterans have to say. People such as Gerald Loeb and Sir John Templeton have shared important investment information about the past with us. Read them and I guarantee you'll be more marketwise.

The good news on the information front is that you can obtain a great deal of investment information either very cheaply or for free. We'll start with the cheapest, most accessible sources, and work up in price from there.

THE BUSINESS PRESS

Canadian newspapers

The Globe and Mail "Report on Business"
The Globe and Mail's national edition varies slightly across the country and the price varies too, but for what this newspaper provides, it's a bargain. The section that does not change from coast to coast is the "Report on Business", and this is what you want to read. The "ROB" is indisputably the number one Canadian daily reference source for general business information. Make no mistake about it, even the busiest executives make time to read it.

Relevant information there includes quotations on what was traded the previous business day, information on annual meetings, reports on press conferences called by companies to make major announcements, and other corporate happenings. Also published are the leading economic indicators, constantly updated: the prime rate, the price of gold, and the value of the Canadian dollar in relation to various world currencies. The staff frequently prepare useful reports comparing the rates on savings and chequing accounts at various financial institutions, GIC rates, and interest-bearing RRSP rates. These charts can save you a considerable amount of time.

What else will you find? More tables, some of which helpfully show the net asset values of a wide range of mutual funds. Even the ads are worth a glance or two. Large ads are placed by companies calling various series of bonds for redemption. There could be a corporate announcement pertinent to your investment plans. Or you might see information on various new products or services. It never hurts to know what is happening at the Banquet Table, even if you choose not to participate.

If you look closely, you'll see that some ads are really corporate press releases, which are known as "tombstones" and display the faces of the latest appointees to the board of directors or of those who have made it into the executive suite.

A company will also run in the "ROB" the final details of a new securities issue so that everyone knows the exact nature of the offering, the final details, and who the underwriters are. All these ads are part of corporations' efforts to get their message out to investors (current and future), to the analysts who advise those investors, and to the industry at large.

The Globe's "ROB" is your daily financial update. Whether or not you read it daily depends on your interest level or the level of your involvement with the market. If you are in the process of becoming an informed investor, it's a good habit to get into. You can bet your broker reads the "ROB" daily.

In 1987, *The Globe and Mail* produced a booklet called *How To Profit from "Report on Business"*. For reprints, the charge is $2. Call (416) 585-5273 or write the Circulation Department, 444 Front Street West, Toronto, Ontario, M2V 2S9 for this valuable reference source.

The Financial Times of Canada

Not to be confused with the British newspaper of the same name, *The Financial Times* is published once a week, on Monday. If you are investigating mutual funds, you should be certain to read it. I find its monthly reports comparing the performance of various mutual funds quite valuable.

"Best Bets" is a section in this newspaper featuring stock recommendations based on analysis of particular companies. You can learn quite a bit by reading why stocks are selected or rejected and then how they perform. Other features cover junior stocks and a weekly market review.

Other articles cover general business matters in greater depth than those in the regular daily press. Special reports examine the outlook and performance of an entire industry or sector. Armed with this knowledge, you are in a better position to evaluate a specific company whose stock you may be interested in purchasing or are already holding.

The same publisher also puts out *Personal Finance*, a monthly booklet with various legal, taxation, and investment strategy articles.

The Financial Post

Once published weekly, *The Financial Post* now comes out daily. In size, it is like *The Financial Times*, but it is substantially different in content. Comprehensive surveys and studies are frequently available in this paper. It covers attitudes about the market, in addition to presenting interviews and descriptions of new developments and products.

The same publisher has a little magazine called *MoneyWise* which comes out once a month. Here is a publication which has many newsy items about people and the market.

All brokerage firms subscribe to The Financial Post Corporation's Service, which provides lots of data in survey form. One part of this service is what are commonly called the Financial Post Cards. These bright yellow cards give all the pertinent data you need about a listed corporation in one handy format. You'll find them in every brokerage library and in major public libraries too.

All three of these Canadian newspapers, plus their associated publications, will give you a good grounding in current events and trends.

Canadian business magazines

Canadian Business
A monthly magazine, *Canadian Business* offers in-depth features on industry trends and regulatory developments and profiles of corporate leaders. In addition, there are regular columns on business developments. Ideal for investors who want to round out their knowledge of what's happening in Canada, it's easy to read, too.

Your Money
Put out by the same people who publish *Canadian Business, Your Money* is geared to smaller investors and concentrates on the many opportunities available to them. *Your Money* offers helpful, useful, and very action-oriented information. It came into the market when you would have thought that it was saturated with business publications, but it has carved out a niche by catering to the individual trying to manage his or her own money.

Industry sources

Toronto Stock Exchange publications
The Toronto Stock Exchange puts out a variety of booklets that are definitely worth reading, and many of them are free. A booklet called *Catalogue of Publications* shows all of the available publications, which include *What Is the TSE 300 Composite Index* and *A Stock Exchange Is. . . .* Call the TSE at (416) 947-4700 or write at The Exchange Tower, 2 First Canadian Place, Toronto, Ontario, M5X 1J2.

CSI Publications
The Canadian Securities Institute, the educational arm of the Canadian Securities Commission, has several informative publications you may want to consider. The list of works runs from *Canadian Mutual Funds* to *How to Invest in Canadian Securities;* the booklet *Investment Terms and Definitions* is definitely a steal at $1.50.
Call (416) 364-9130 or write to CSI at 33 Yonge Street, Suite 360, Toronto, Ontario, M5E 1G4.

US business press
The Wall Street Journal, Barron's, Forbes, Business Week, and *Fortune* are just some of

the better known names among US business publications. This list of publications is by no means exhaustive, but it gives you a starting point. If you are looking at a particular industry, you should also explore the field's trade publications. One way to do this is to ask the business-section librarian for recommendations. To give an example, let's say you are convinced that grocery-related stocks are going to be a good bet and currently offer a stock market bargain. Try reading *Canadian Grocer* — a periodical for the trade. Most industries have at least one trade magazine. Often there is a Canadian and an American trade journal, both of which are worth reading.

One caution: if you can read all of these you will be incredibly knowledgeable, but you probably won't have slept for a week. (This is where speed reading really is an asset!)

MY RECOMMENDED STRATEGY: When you're starting out, review all these publications, but look at library copies. If you find one that you learn from consistently, you can subscribe so that you don't miss a single issue. But don't do what a friend of mine did and order wildly until you reach the saturation point. She would groan every time another publication came in the mail. Try before you buy. There is no point in buying what you won't have time to read. Set aside a regular time to read publications. (By going to the library you may get that moment of peace you need to concentrate.)

Keep in mind that as you become a more sophisticated investor, you will discover that the hottest information is often stale once it has reached the magazines. A magazine takes as much as three months to prepare. Even in these days of computer-assisted publishing the bulk of an article is generally prepared long before it appears on the stands. Therefore the pieces carried are not likely to cause a thunderbolt of activity in a particular sector. There are exceptions, but in general you should treat these articles as background research, not as news. To have broad knowledge you need to look at both daily news and lengthy business articles.

CORPORATE INFORMATION

Never take anything at face value is probably a good motto when it comes to corporate information. Why such a cautious approach? Every corporation has interests which it tries to promote. To protect your own interests, you must learn to separate the facts from the public relations. You must be able to read between the lines.

Most public companies are happy to send you information. Annual reports, quarterly reports, a complete information package — all can be yours if you write or phone the company and say that you are considering becoming a shareholder. When you write or call a company, be sure to address yourself to the shareholder division or the public relations department. If you are very interested, ask if the firm has a mailing list and if your name could be placed on it.

If you have access to a major library, you can obtain valuable reference material. Annual reports and corporate files, publications of the Financial Post Corporation Service, and more are available in the business section of sizeable libraries.

Briefly, the first and essential step to understanding corporate data is to learn how to read a balance sheet and an income statement. It is really quite easy. The income statement reveals a company's health by telling you how it performed during the most recent year compared to the previous year and how much of a profit or loss it showed. The balance sheet gives you additional perspective on the income statement by showing what the company owns and what it owes. Never, never ignore the footnotes in any financial report you read.

The only tip on reading reports that I'll offer here is: *always watch for the cash flow*. You determine cash flow by finding the company's net earnings and adding back any deductions, such as depreciation, that are not paid out in actual dollars.

Many good books on interpreting financial reports are available, so I won't go into further detail here. Your broker's firm may put out a brochure designed to help you with this. If not, the one I recommend for everyone is the Canadian Securities Institute's introductory guide, *How To Read a Financial Statement*, which is available at a minimal cost.

When you start to read the business press you may initially feel overwhelmed. Most people are. So at the beginning, focus on a particular publication or a particular industry to start developing your investment knowledge. Master this, and move on to your next interest. Balance keeping informed about current events and gaining a long-term perspective in order to get the full flavour of the investment world.

RESEARCH

Publications
The *Investor's Digest of Canada* is a bi-weekly news sheet offering extensive analyses by various investment dealers. Periodically, it presents "The Forecaster", a forum in which investment houses project earnings for individual stocks. Keep in mind that by the time subscribers receive the *Investor's Digest*, the information is not hot off the presses. At the least, it has already gone from the analysts to their firm's brokers and out to their clients. Never mind, it is still very useful because it shows you what a range of analysts are recommending about stocks or industries. Besides, if they happen to have been early in their predictions, they'll save you money. Look for this publication in the library.

Brokers' research
If a particular stock or analyst's opinion catches your eye, phone that investment firm directly and request a copy of the research report. Keep in mind when you do this, though, that you will be contacted later by a broker from the firm to see if the material was useful to you and to discuss your thoughts on investing. This won't be a social call. Research is part of a brokerage house's marketing effort, sent out to generate business. So don't expect to receive an unlimited amount of free research from the brokerage houses unless you conduct some business with them. It would be unrealistic to expect unlimited research at no cost.

One reason for brokers' sensitivity on the question of the distribution of research is the appearance of discount brokers. Some clients take research material from a full-service broker and act on it with a discount broker. This seems unjust to those firms that pay analysts in their research departments.

As I mentioned in Chapter Four, discount brokers provide fewer services than full-service brokers, with a commensurate lower cost. My own feeling about discount brokers is that they play a very important role in our marketplace. If you do your own research and do not require advice and service from a broker, why should you pay for this in your commissions? Just as you can choose to bag your own groceries or buy from a catalogue at reduced rates, you should have the option of selecting a discount broker. Most investors want personal attention and information from their brokers, but those who do not should not have to pay for a service they don't use.

Informal information networking
Since we have raised the subject of research and discount brokers, let's look again at what you can expect from your broker. On the way to becoming an informed investor, you'll probably find advantages in having someone with whom you can discuss your plans and prospects. You can get a lot of information from your broker this way, although, as I mentioned earlier, you must remember that your broker's time is limited and try to keep the conversations concise.

You can definitely benefit from the network your broker has established professionally. If you inquire about a promising stock, your broker can probably locate some relevant information for you. He or she is not a researcher but does sit surrounded by quote machines, colleagues who may have other sources of information they'll share, and a corporate library filled with material. In addition, your broker probably has a sales assistant, and it is possible to request information from this person.

Some brokers supply you with tons of additional information. Some don't, which doesn't mean that they are negligent. You could drown in all the available information. Are additional details really that vital to you? If not, then the short and sweet version of the story may be enough. Also, thousands of stocks are available, a research team cannot follow all of them.

Here's an example of how a broker's network functions, and how you can make this information exchange work for you.

Let's say your broker calls to tell you about a real estate tax shelter. Swiftly you ask for and receive the brochure on the project. You get some information about this development from the glossy publication, but you may find yourself thinking that this looks too good to be true.

You've read the brochure, but how do you get further information? You could use your own resources to check further. Be inventive. Find a contact — a friend, a business associate, or someone you know to be an expert in the area. You simply call up one of these people on the telephone and seek advice.

I use this example because this is exactly what happened to me. A client mentioned the project to me, and I called a friend in the real estate business who just happened to know the location. "No way," she said, "that's right near an institution, in a poor location, with little chance of appreciation, and the area is . . . ." In short, in her opinion, the whole project wasn't what it first appeared to be. You should try to check or have someone else check if possible.

HOW TO BENEFIT FROM METHODS USED BY BIG-TIME INVESTORS

Now let's look at how professional money managers gather their information. I'm not suggesting you follow these examples exactly, but the marketwise investor should know how the professionals do it. Then you can adapt those methods to suit your own information-gathering techniques.

Economic forecasting

The first steps for the experts is to absorb huge quantities of information from a wide variety of sources in order to understand what the economy is doing. This is called the top-down approach. Before deciding on specific investment action, it's necessary to determine what the whole economy is doing.

The place to start is with the known facts. You may have heard of economic indicators. These straightforward data can be of great assistance once you learn how to use them.

Indicators are signs that tell you in a capsule form what is happening in the economy. It's like the weather: a forecast tells you what the experts think will happen, temperature and barometer reading tell you what is happening, and the evening weather report sums up what has happened. In much the same way, economic indicators tell you the economic weather.

Economic indicators are of three basic types: leading, lagging, and co-incident. (Readers with math or economics anxiety should take a deep breath and refuse to be thrown off by the jargon. It will all be explained.)

- You are already familiar with the Toronto Stock Exchange 300 index, which indicates the value of 300 (out of the more than a thousand) stocks on the Toronto Stock Exchange and its daily movements. This is known as a *leading indicator* because it is thought to reveal economic trends before they occur. This means that by following the progress of the TSE index, some analysts believe that you can make predictions about the future behaviour of the economy. So, for example, they think that a fairly steady downward movement of the index signals a coming slowdown in the economy.

- *Coincident indicators* give an instant reading of the phenomena they describe, just as a thermometer gives you the current temperature reading. For example, unemployment rates are coincident indicators. They tend to confirm that a prediction about the behaviour of the economy is correct (as opposed to offering much warning for the future).

- Finally, a *lagging indicator* is one that occurs after the economic event. One example is data on capital spending. If a number of companies have good sales and good earnings, they likely have the money to put into a new plant and equipment. But the figures for such an indicator are not compiled before the economic event is achieved; thus, they lag what they show, tending to confirm an economic event which has passed.

The indicators themselves offer straightforward statistics, and few people argue about their overall accuracy. What people do argue about is what the indicators mean. You probably know many variations on the joke about economists and analysts: they all reach different conclusions based on the same data. For example the stock market is considered to be a three- to six-month leading indicator; however, it is not always easy to decipher what it was trying to tell you until after the fact.

Nevertheless, the professional money managers look at these and many more indicators and information in order to arrive at an economic forecast and thus an investment scenario. This is what makes them more informed than others who stick with a few details and ignore the larger picture. Time is crucial for the pros. Their interpretation of what is happening is always expressed in terms of short-, medium-, and long-range outlooks.

Understanding this frame of reference is very important. If you know how it is done, you are in a much better position to assess the forecasts you receive and to have a basis for forming your own opinions. In this fast-changing world, I promise you that nothing is more valuable than timely information and a frame of reference. Mastering these techniques makes you less of a follower and less likely to be misled.

What happens after I get the big picture?
Forming this big picture can be aided by using other indicators, such as inflation, interest and exchange rates, net exports, the deficit, and more forecasts of the lot. Keep in mind that you don't need to cope with all this daily. If you check these indicators and the forecasts summarizing trends every three months, you can generally stay on top of the situation. Remember the reading you are doing? *The Globe and Mail's* "ROB" features these figures, and business magazines and *The Financial Times* or *Financial Post* carry updates that are easily accessible.

When the experts have a general frame of reference, they apply it to specific sectors. When you receive a research report from your broker on an industry — forest products for example — this framework was the starting point. Then other factors relevant to the industry in question were added. For example, the trade dispute with the United States in 1987 meant that the political environment had a serious and very direct impact on the forest products industry and its investment opportunities.

This large view is linked to specific action by means of an implied question: if this economic view proves correct, what sectors will benefit? For example, if the analyst's large view is that inflation will decline, consumer spending could improve because the dollar will have more purchasing power. In this scenario companies that produce or sell consumer goods, such as retailers, should be the winners.

Thus, when reading the experts, you'll find that they tend to begin with observations on the overall economy and market and the direction they feel we are moving. Then they get down to the nitty gritty of stock recommendations. These recommendations all hinge on the base from which they build their forecasts, their specific economic assumptions about inflation and interest rates and so on.

But as I mentioned, the analysts frequently don't agree. I will never forget a week when three investment firms issued reports: one was bullish on the market; the second was bearish; and the third said that it would be flat, without real movement up or down. It is at times like these that you are well-advised to understand the indicators and try to form your own conclusions.

Try to get comfortable with the frustrating fact that experts don't always agree. When you understand how analysis works, you can see why there is so much room for disagreement. The best attitude is a straight facing of the facts. Try to avoid wishful thinking or the kind of ego investment that turns every market encounter into a test of who called it right and who called it wrong.

As with tennis or golf, you can improve your game by watching how the pros do it. In one of my favourite books, *The Money Masters*, John Train profiles nine leading money managers and tells how they do it. Reading this book should definitely be profitable to you.

Once the experts gather economic information, what kind of general analysis do they apply? Can you make use of these methods?

I'll discuss three approaches: fundamental, technical, and what I call psychological.

Fundamental analysis

This is the approach you normally read about in the paper and the one used by most research analysts. They take the numbers released by companies and calculate various ratios from them in order to analyse corporate performance. A good booklet, as I mentioned earlier, is put out by the Canadian Securities Institute under the title *How to Read a Financial Statement*.

EXHIBIT 11.1
Trans-Canada Retail Stores Limited
Consolidated Balance Sheet

ASSETS

CURRENT ASSETS

1. Cash and bank balances .... $ 129,000
2. Marketable securities — at cost, which approximates market value 2,040,000
3. Accounts receivable (less allowances for doubtful accounts — $9,000)...... 975,000
4. Inventories of merchandise — valued at the lower of cost or market 9,035,000
5. Prepaid expenses...... 59,000
6.   Total Current Assets $12,238,000

MISCELLANEOUS ASSET

7. Investment in affiliated company 917,000

8. FIXED ASSETS, at cost
   Buildings $2,460,000
   Equipment 6,750,000
                   9,210,000
   Accumulated depreciation 4,260,000   4,950,000
   Land 1,370,000

9. DEFERRED CHARGES
   (unamortized expenses and discount
   on bond issue)...... 136,000

INTANGIBLE ASSET

10. Goodwill	1
11.	$19,611,001

LIABILITIES

CURRENT LIABILITIES

12. Bank advances	$ 1,630,000
13. Accounts payable	2,165,000
14. Dividends payable	97,000
15. Income taxes payable	398,000
16. First mortgage bonds due within one year	240,000
17. Total Current Liabilities	$ 4,530,000
18. DEFERRED INCOME TAXES	485,000
19. MINORITY INTEREST IN SUBSIDIARY COMPANIES	157,000

FUNDED DEBT (due after one year)

20. 5½% First Mortgage Sinking Fund Bonds due December 30, 19••	2,700,000

SHAREHOLDERS' EQUITY

CAPITAL STOCK

21. $2.50 Cumulative Redeemable Preferred — Authorized 20,000 shares, $50 par value — issued and outstanding 15,000 shares	750,000
22. Common — Authorized 500,000 shares of no par value — issued and outstanding 350,000 shares	1,564,000
23. CONTRIBUTED SURPLUS	210,000
24. RETAINED EARNINGS	9,215,001
	11,739,001
25.	$19,611,001

Canadian Securities Institute

Exhibit 11.1 shows "Trans-Canada Retail Stores Limited's" balance sheet.

One of the first ratios the analysts calculate is the price/earnings (P/E) ratio. It is calculated by taking the current price of the stock and dividing it by the annual earnings per share. They then repeat the calculation using the projected future earnings.

Let's say, for example, an analyst knows that a company's per-share earnings are $1.00 this year and are projected to be $1.20 next year and $1.45 the following year. The analyst then calculates the P/E ratio, current and projected, based on the current stock price — say $10:

$$\$10 \div \$1.00 = 10.0$$
$$\$10 \div \$1.20 = 8.3$$
$$\$10 \div \$1.45 = 6.9$$

But if the P/E ratio for this stock has generally been 10 and the $1.45 earnings estimate comes to pass in two years, then the stock will trade at

$$\$1.45 \times 10 = \$14.50$$

Thus, the stock looks cheap now compared to the price the analysts feel it could reach in a year or two, so perhaps it's a good opportunity.

Analysts use more than 20 ratios on the balance sheet and the income statement, both of which are found in every company's annual report and financial statements. The ratios tell you whether a company's financial health is declining or improving. Another reason ratios are important is because they give a basis for comparison. By comparing the ratios of different companies you can see whether a company is in line with others in the same industry. If it is out of line, a research analyst can check and tell you why.

One advantage of using the *Investor's Digest* is that it presents industry-wide surveys of ratios, based on research reports from various brokerage houses. That can save you a lot of calculation time, and the results may be more complete than what you can come up with. After all, analysts spend their whole day combing through company information and comparing facts as they look for bargains for their firm's clients.

From the balance sheet figures, the income statement, and the footnotes to the financial report, analysts extract information to tell the story. On the basis of this information and its interpretation, which is rooted in general economic forecasts, they can recommend investment decisions.

MY RECOMMENDED STRATEGY: Analysts at many brokerage firms have difficulty writing the word "sell". If they think you should buy, they say so in plain words, but sell is usually phrased in less clear-cut language. No company wants its stock rated a sell, and an analyst runs the risk of being in the company's bad books if he or she makes such a recommendation. Therefore you need to interpret some jargon. In broker talk, "sell" may be stated as "looks fully priced here" or "hold for the long term".

"Hold" is another interesting word. It doesn't mean sell, and it doesn't mean buy. What are we holding for?

Most analysts at brokerage firms are fundamentalists. One simple reason is that any recommendations made must be backed up with facts and figures, since vast sums of money are involved. Keep in mind, it all starts with learning to read corporate financial statements. Although you have probably chosen a career other than that of an analyst, it is in your best interest to understand the basis for the recommendations.

Technical analysis
The technical analysts, sometimes called chartists, look at charts and interpret the meaning of the patterns. Riddled with jargon, the technical analyst's method is completely

different from that of the fundamentalist. The idea is that the study of the historical movements of key information can reveal patterns and suggest action to take.

When chartists look at the entire history of the TSE index, the Dow Jones index, inflation rates, interest rates, or stock prices presented on charts, they are looking for patterns. Based on their study of previous patterns, they try to discern a buy, a sell, or a stay-put recommendation.

Among the types of graphs or charts technical analysts use are point and figure graphs, bar graphs, and graphs containing advance and decline lines. To give you some idea of the intricacies, here are some of the names given various patterns: double top, triple top, head and shoulders, and reverse head and shoulders. If you want to see more, you should read a publication called *Graphoscope*, which publishes daily, weekly, and monthly charts. You can find it in the library or order it by writing to GPS Publishing Ltd., 30 Duncan Street, Toronto, Ontario, M5V 2C3.

Helpful hint: Technical analysts also have difficulty writing the word "sell". If you read that a stock has "topped out", interpret this to mean "sell it".

An important person in the field of technical analysis is Norman G. Fosback, who has written a comprehensive book called *Stock Market Logic*. Unfortunately, this excellent book is available only when you buy his newsletter. If you want to try the granddaddy of technical analysis, read Robert D. Edwards and John Magee's *Technical Analysis of Stock Trends*, or the 600-page book *How the Average Investor Can Use Technical Analysis for Stock Profits,* by James Dines.

You may have heard about various theoretical versions of the chartist approach, such as the Elliott wave theory. Robert Prechter spreads the word according to Elliott and has enjoyed substantial success in his predictions. His publication is called *The Elliott Wave Theorist*, and you can write for more information to New Classics Library Inc., P.O. Box 1618, Gainsville, Georgia, U.S.A. 30503. In Canada, one of the leading chartists is Toronto-based Ian McAvity. He writes a publication called *Deliberations*, which you can obtain by telephoning (416) 867-1100.

Technical analysts number only few, but I have always found it interesting that many fundamental analysts ask for a technical view on their recommendations just to confirm their opinions. Technicians bring such factors as investor sentiment and economic cycles into their forecasting.

MY RECOMMENDED STRATEGY: We know that the world of investment information has always been more art than science. Don't try to pick stocks by yourself using technical analysis. It looks easy, but it is very complex. Rely on the experts who have had years of training.

Psychological analysis
Psychological analysis is yet another approach. It asks why people are doing what they're doing. It looks at crowd behaviour. It means using *your* powers of prediction. I consider this approach a valuable addition to the more traditional methods, which sometimes tend to take a logical approach (analysing) to an illogical item (the market), as Bennett Goodspeed says in his book, *The Tao Jones Averages.*

Psychological analysts, often called contrarians, takes the view that there is a large psychological (meaning unknown or uncontrollable) component to investor behaviour. "What's the feeling towards investment in forestry, mining, manufacturing, and so on?" they ask. In other words, what will investors buy in certain sectors based on the current environment? Although a company may look good on the fundamental front (the ratios), the mood of investors towards that specific industry may be bad. Perhaps there's scepticism about the rate of growth a company is experiencing or something just seems not right.

I feel there is a strong case for psychological analysis. The market can move quickly on rumours. A stock may go up or down without any change in the facts. It seems inexplicable. Perhaps psychological perceptions, not the market or the numbers, are driving the stock. The case of companies with investments in South Africa in late 1987 is an example. There was no change in the fundamentals of this diverse group of companies, but some investors chose to sell their holdings. Social and political factors can have an obvious impact on how a stock is perceived.

The psychological approach involves a certain amount of "what if" thinking. What if interest rates go down? What if inflation rises? What if the political scene changes? Trends spring up and disappear like hemlines (which used to be a favourite market indicator). This year the trend may be oil stocks, and next year it might be computer stocks. Can you figure out what's next?

Sometimes when you're assessing a stock, you simply have a feeling that an idea will work. When we talk about an analyst's gut feeling, the gut we are talking about is probably an educated gut. Someone who has been in business or around the market for a long time learns to develop intuition and instincts. But you have assessment powers too, and maybe you will spot a trend based on your own observations.

In many ways, it seems to me, the renowned American investor, Sir John Templeton, uses psychological analysis as part of his investment approach. He never buys a stock which is currently popular. He calls his method Value Investing, but it contains elements of contrarian investment, which boils down to buying what other's don't currently find interesting. In fact, one book he recommends is *Extraordinary Popular Delusions and the Madness of Crowds,* written by Charles Mackay in 1841.

The Contrarian Approach
Being a contrarian and using a psychological approach are not always the same thing although they do have one common element: using your gut instinct and not just looking at today's numbers.

The contrarian strategy is outlined in David Dreman's book *The New Contrarian Investment*. The contrarian buys a stock because he or she feels that in the future someone will consider it worthwhile and will want to pay more for it — maybe a lot more.

The central idea of contrarian investment is reflected in its name, which signifies going against the grain. You buy stocks cheaply, perhaps with little current fundamental evidence for the soundness of the investment decision. Then you hold on to them until they improve and, cross your fingers, reveal the potential that you saw all along. A good example was the purchase of Noranda shares when the company fell on hard times in the recession. The fundamental numbers were bad. The firm had big debt, it was highly leveraged, there was talk of bankruptcy. On a chart, it looked like a nose dive. But some people were buying the stock while it declined. Why? Because they felt that the down trend in prices would reverse. The potential for increase was greater there than in other companies that were available and perhaps highly recommended for purchase. These contrarians proved to have guessed right about Noranda; the stock recovered in 1986 and 1987 and yielded substantial returns.

The contrarian looks for the opportunity to bet on the underdog. A choice may not be easily justified on fundamentals or on a chart, but the marketwise investor examines the facts, risk and reward, and then decides to proceed. With contrarian investment, buying stocks when they are low often means reduced risk because the stocks usually don't have that much farther to fall since they're down in price already.

Contrarian stock-picking is like buying a winter coat on sale at the tail end of the season, knowing that although no one wants one now people will be buying them again in the future. The contrarian view is long range and anti-popular. To take this type of approach, you can't be eager for action right away. It could take several years for your forecast to be realized. Contrarian investing is an attitude — a bargain-hunting attitude. You don't care whether others are buying today or not, in fact, you rather hope they aren't. Instead of following the crowd, you follow your hunch. But keep in mind what I said about the educated gut. I'm not talking about buying junk, rather about buying value according to a strategy. You may have to work up to this method of investing.

Here's an example of how this approach paid off for Barbara, one of my clients. Barbara worked for an advertising company at a time when it was doing work for the *Toronto Sun*. No one was highly recommending the newspaper's stock at that time, but Barbara was very impressed with the management group she was meeting there. Her gut told her that this company was going places. Although fairly new to the market, she decided to trust her instinct. She purchased the stock at $7, and it moved up in value five times over the years (see Exhibit 11.2). There is a terrific example of how a gutsy move paid off handsomely. She then did the same thing with Cadillac Fairview stock.

Now every contrarian story does not have the same happy ending as Barbara's. After all, there is a risk. But you do not have to follow the crowd. You must be prepared to think for yourself and to develop your investment instincts. Respect yourself enough not to get too self-assured too soon. Start educating yourself today so that you can recognize a great opportunity when it comes your way.

If you want a broker who takes this type of approach, start by talking about philosophy of investment. Outline your own philosophy to your prospective broker early in the working relationship and make sure that you are in tune with one another. Then instruct him or her to go after bargains, longer range situations, and other contrarian opportunities. Even a broker who doesn't use this approach totally may accept that you are interested in it and be willing to keep an eye out for opportunities so that you can achieve the results you are after.

EXHIBIT 11.2
Toronto Sun Stock Purchase Chart

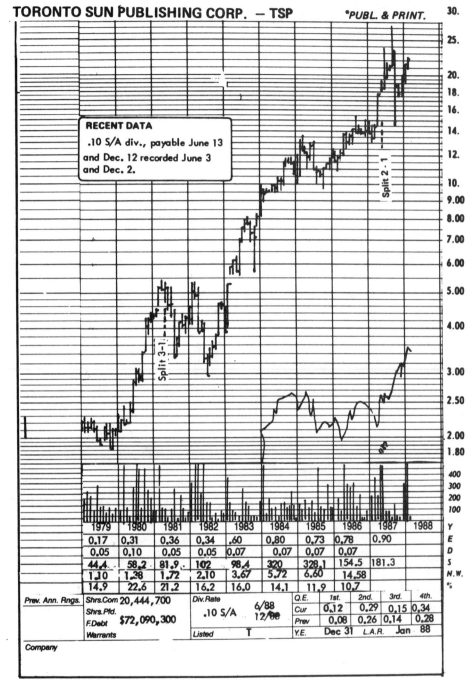

Graphoscope

Remember information is everywhere. It is how you use and interpret it that counts. Of course, if none of this research interests you at all, you should find a stockbroker whom it does interest.

In this chapter we looked at
     — many different sources of reading material about the business world,
     — research publications,
     — fundamental, technical, and psychological analysis,
     — where to find more information.

This was another information-packed section you'll want to refer to again. Meanwhile, we'll move on to the next chapter, which outline the actions you need to take to keep right on top of things after you become an investor.

Chapter Twelve

AFTER TAKING THE PLUNGE: NOW WHAT DO I DO?

Okay, you took the giant step and bought securities. Where do you go from here? Some investors experience trauma after they buy stocks because they don't know what to do next. Some also wonder if they've done the right thing. About three days after a purchase, some people experience buyer's remorse — the "Oh no, what have I done?" feeling of regret. That's normal, so try not to let it bother you.

You do, however, want to make sure that you are doing everything you can as a participant in the stock market. So in this chapter, we shall examine what can happen to your securities and what you can do about it.

WHEN DO I PAY FOR MY SHARES?
In an earlier chapter, we discussed how to buy stocks. After the purchase, you receive in the mail a confirmation which gives the details of your purchase. Payment must be received at the firm's office within five business days of this purchase. You are responsible for this payment, whether the postal system is having a good week or not, and you will be charged interest if your money is received after the due date. So don't wait for the confirmation to arrive before sending the money in. The best practice is to call your broker and find out the total amount due.

If you wish to hold your stock certificates yourself (more on this in a minute), don't expect to pick them up right away. It can take six to eight weeks for shares to be registered in your name.

WHERE SHOULD I KEEP MY SECURITIES?
You have two choices for storing your securities, and there are pros and cons to each. You can keep the certificates in a safety deposit box or you can leave them with your broker.

If you take possession of the certificates, you must register your shares in your own name and *put them in a safety deposit box*. Don't even consider keeping them in a drawer at home. It invites danger. The cost of renting a safety deposit box is a tax-deductible expense so there is no financial reason for keeping the certificates at home. If you lose one, the replacement cost and procedure are a nightmare. It takes three to six months to replace a certificate, and during that period you cannot sell your stock because the ownership has to be reconfirmed. Also, beginning the replacement procedure can cost you 3 to 4% of the value of the lost stock. In other words, it's a big expensive pain.

If you decide to take possession of the certificates, it is essential that you send any change of address to the transfer agent (the name and address keeper) so that you will continue to receive up-to-date information. This is your responsibility. If you are receiving dividends, you have an extra incentive since you don't want the cheque getting lost or delayed going to the wrong address.

If you decide to store your securities with your broker, you choose one of two options. First, they can be held in what is called *registered form*, which means they are registered in your name. The dividends and annual reports come directly to your home address. The brokerage simply provides storage, normally for a safekeeping charge. (In fact, because of high administrative costs, some firms will not allow you to take this course.)

More commonly, stocks kept at a brokerage house are in *street form*. That is, they are registered not in your name but in the brokerage's name. There is generally no cost to you for keeping your shares in street form. Your certificates are insured against loss. The firm keeps a record of them and sends you frequent statements reporting your holdings. If dividends are paid in your name, they are deposited into your account on the correct payment date. If shareholders are sent important notices, such as news of an impending stock split, or rights issue, they go to your broker, who will call you.

Most brokerage firms prefer you to leave the stock with them in street form.

Doing this also provides considerable convenience to you. If you move, you will need to make only one change of address to the brokerage firm to keep all of the records straight instead of having to write to the transfer agent of every company in which you own shares. If you trade frequently, you are better served by keeping your shares with the brokerage firm. Otherwise, you must forever troop to the safety deposit box and take the share certificates to your broker. If you don't live close to your broker, you can find yourself sending quite a bit of registered mail.

Keep in mind, though, what you don't get if you keep your shares in street form with your broker. For US securities, you will not receive the annual report or the quarterly financial statements unless you make special provision with the company or with your broker to receive them. For Canadian securities, you have the option to receive or not to receive any company correspondence. Because the registered owner of the shares is the brokerage firm, it always receives the reports.

By choosing one method or the other of storage, you are not making an irrevocable decision. You can always change your mind.

WHAT CAN I DO WITH MY DIVIDENDS?

If your shares are held with the brokerage firm, dividends received are deposited into your account. You can set up your account so that this money is mailed out to you when it arrives. Many investors find, however, that the better way to make their money grow is to keep the dividends in their investment account, and earmark these funds for investment purposes. After all, what can you do with a cheque for $26? Most people spend it. If you leave it in your investment account, you have all of your investment capital in one place.

PAINLESS PORTFOLIO BUILDING 3

The discussion of dividends brings me to the third *Painless Portfolio Building* idea. Previously we looked at ways in which you could painlessly build up your portfolio using Canada Savings Bonds and mutual funds. Now let's look at the dividend reinvestment plan.

Approximately 50 major corporations offer a special feature known as the dividend reinvestment plan. Bell Canada Enterprises, Imperial Oil, bank stocks, steel companies, and utility companies are some examples of corporations offering this terrific plan. Generally, you need to own 100 shares to start one of these plans.

Let's look at an example. If you own 100 shares of a stock paying out a $2 annual dividend per share, every quarter you receive a cheque calculated like this:

$$\$2 \div 4 \text{ quarters } = \$0.50 \text{ per share per quarter}$$
$$\$0.50 \times 100 \text{ shares } = \$50.00$$

Most people just toss a $50 cheque into the general pot and spend it.

Why not try something different? Since you own shares in this company already, you obviously feel positively about it and would consider owning more. Why not add to your position? In a dividend reinvestment plan, the company puts your dividend towards buying those additional shares for you.

The plan has three extra attractive features.

- It's very convenient. You don't have to do anything except sign a form stating you want to be on the dividend reinvestment plan. Your $50 dividend cheque goes to buy more shares of the company. If the shares are trading at $40, you will be credited with 1.25 shares:

$$\$50 \text{ dividend } \div \$40 = 1.25 \text{ shares}$$

You could not do this in the regular marketplace, since fractional shares are not available. Moreover, when you receive your next quarterly dividend, it will be calculated on the basis of ownership of 101 full shares (no fraction allowed here), so you get $50.50 to buy more shares.

In effect, your shares are compounding and growing as your money continually gets reinvested into the company. The company will send you an updated record each quarter of what you now own, including the fractions which are growing into whole shares.

- A second benefit is that no commission is charged for shares bought with the dividend reinvestment plan. The company is happy that you are buying more of its shares. Many companies will allow you to add money to the dividend amount and purchase even more shares for no commission. The company is encouraging you to buy more and reinvest with them. The cost saving to you is tremendous.

- Several companies offering dividend reinvestment plans issue the extra shares to you at a 5% discount to the market price, making the plan even more attractive. (Reinvestment is a way in which the company conserves money to put it to good use.)

You must sign up to benefit from a dividend reinvestment plan, and to do that, your shares must be registered in your name, not your broker's. If your shares are currently registered in the brokerage firm's name, have your broker transfer them to your name. As I said before, registering securities takes six to eight weeks, so plan ahead.

Also, if you take advantage of this method of building your portfolio, you must plan ahead if you want to sell. You are not actually issued the shares you buy each quarter on the dividend reinvestment plan. When you are ready to sell or to stop the plan, you notify the company of your decision and it will issue you the certificate for the extra shares that you have purchased. It takes about a month to get them to you. You need to have the certificates in your possession before you can sell, so you must plan ahead.

Here's an example of a marketwise investor who was looking for a painless way to build her portfolio. My client, Irene, bought 100 Bell Canada shares at $19.00 per share on October 1, 1982. Exibit 12.1 shows her progress over the course of two years participating in that company's dividend reinvestment plan. As you can see, she increased her share ownership by 18.763 shares by January 16, 1985. She was also taking advantage of the dollar-cost averaging I spoke of in Chapter Eight.

WHAT HAPPENS IF MY SHARES SPLIT?

A stock splits when a company divides the outstanding shares into a larger number of shares. A three-for-one split by a company with 1 million shares outstanding results in 3 million shares outstanding. If you held 100 shares before the split, you now hold 300 shares. You hold the same proportion of ownership in the company as you held before the split. Only the number of shares and the corresponding prices have changed.

Why does a company split its stock? Perhaps its shares have a high market price; there is psychologically more interest in a share trading at $20 than $60. A three-for-one split brings down the share price to one-third of its former cost and perhaps makes it more accessible to investors.

If a company in which you own stock announces a split, what should you watch out for? First of all, after a stock split the price of the shares often rises. Take the earlier example of a three-for-one split of stock that has been trading at $60 per share. Instead of going down to $20, it may trade at $20⅛ or $20¼. One reason may be more interest in and access to the shares at the lower price. In general, a stock split is good news for investors and is well received in the marketplace. Often the share price has initially gone up so high because of good financial news and continues to go up after the split.

A stock may also go through a reverse split. Say, 100 million shares are outstanding, trading at $0.35 and management decides to consolidate in a one-for-ten reverse split. If you owned 1000 shares, you now own 100.

A reverse split can also be good news. It means that the company is trying to tighten up the number of shares issued; in the example, you now theoretically have 100 shares

EXHIBIT 12.1
An Example of Portfolio Building
with a Dividend Reinvestment Plan

The Treasurer
Bell Canada Enterprises Inc.
P.O. Box 6074, Stn A
Montreal, Quebec, H3C 3G4
Telephone (514) 870-6251

SHAREHOLDER DIVIDEND REINVESTMENT AND STOCK PURCHASE PLAN

STATEMENT OF ACCOUNT   Date 27/07/83

Account No.   **COMMON SHARE DIVIDENDS REINVESTED**   **PAGE 1**

Record Date	Payment Date	Dividend Rate	Shares held by you	Shares held in DRP	Net Dividend
15/06/83	15/07/83	.52	100	4.4837	54.34

TRANSACTIONS

DATE	CODE	COMMON DIVIDEND ACTIVITY $	TOTAL COMMON DIVIDEND $	CASH ACTIVITY $	TOTAL CASH HELD FOR REINVESTMENT $	PRICE PER SHARE $	SHARES PURCHASED/WITHDRAWN	SHARES HELD IN DRP
15/01/83	DC	52.00	52.00		0.00			0.0000
17/01/83	PD	−52.00	0.00		0.00	22.6218	2.2987	2.2987
15/04/83	DP	1.19	1.19		0.00			2.2987
15/04/83	DC	52.00	53.19		0.00			2.2987
18/04/83	PD	−53.19	0.00		0.00	24.3437	2.1850	4.4837
15/07/83	DP	2.34	2.34		0.00			4.4837
15/07/83	DC	52.00	54.34		0.00			4.4837
18/07/83	PD	−54.34	0.00		0.00	24.7831	2.1926	6.6763

Shareholder Dividend Reinvestment and Stock Purchase Plan ("DRP")

STATEMENT OF ACCOUNT

Date 27/10/84

Account No.   **COMMON SHARE DIVIDENDS REINVESTED**   **PAGE 1**

Record Date	Payment Date	Dividend Rate	Shares held by you	Shares held in DRP	Net Dividend
14/09/84	15/10/84	.545	100	14.7676	62.55

TRANSACTIONS

DATE	CODE	COMMON DIVIDEND ACTIVITY $	TOTAL COMMON DIVIDEND $	CASH ACTIVITY $	TOTAL CASH HELD FOR REINVESTMENT $	PRICE PER SHARE $	SHARES PURCHASED/WITHDRAWN	SHARES HELD IN DRP
28/10/83	AC		0.00		0.00			8.6406
15/01/84	DP	4.71	4.71		0.00			8.6406
15/01/84	DC	54.50	59.21		0.00			8.6406
16/01/84	PD	−59.21	0.00		0.00	30.5781	1.9364	10.5770
15/04/84	DP	5.77	5.77		0.00			10.5770
15/04/84	DC	54.50	60.27		0.00			10.5770
16/04/84	PD	−60.27	0.00		0.00	27.8825	2.1616	12.7386
15/07/84	DP	6.94	6.94		0.00			12.7386
15/07/84	DC	54.50	61.44		0.00			12.7386
16/07/84	PD	−61.44	0.00		0.00	30.2812	2.0290	14.7676
15/10/84	DP	8.05	8.05		0.00			14.7676
15/10/84	DC	54.50	62.55		0.00			14.7676
16/10/84	PD	−62.55	0.00		0.00	31.6112	1.9788	16.7464

Shareholder Dividend Reinvestment and Stock Purchase Plan ("DRP")

STATEMENT OF ACCOUNT

Date 29/01/95

Account No.   **COMMON SHARE DIVIDENDS REINVESTED**   **PAGE 1**

Record Date	Payment Date	Dividend Rate	Shares held by you	Shares held in DRP	Net Dividend
14/12/84	15/01/85	.570	100	16.7464	66.55

TRANSACTIONS

DATE	CODE	COMMON DIVIDEND ACTIVITY $	TOTAL COMMON DIVIDEND $	CASH ACTIVITY $	TOTAL CASH HELD FOR REINVESTMENT $	PRICE PER SHARE $	SHARES PURCHASED/WITHDRAWN	SHARES HELD IN DRP
29/10/84	AC		0.00		0.00			16.7464
15/01/85	DP	9.55	9.55		0.00			16.7464
15/01/85	DC	57.00	66.55		0.00			16.7464
16/01/85	PD	−66.55	0.00		0.00	33.0006	2.0166	18.7630

Bell Canada Enterprises Inc.

trading at $3.50. I must warn you, though, that when a stock moves from being priced as a penny stock to a junior stock, it loses a certain speculative appeal. The company is undergoing a transformation. Also, the "price" change doesn't always improve its performance. The company may have been financially weak from the outset.

What should you do if your stock splits? A split is generally a good sign that the company you picked is going somewhere, so you may just want to continue holding.

HELP! I'M BEING TAKEN OVER!

Another event in the life of a shareholder is a takeover bid. If you discover one day that, without warning, your shares in a company are substantially increasing in price with a high volume of shares being traded, a takeover may be underway. There could be another explanation, such as pending corporate news, but maybe someone wants to buy your company.

The next indication of a takeover could be a halt trading request (by the company being taken over, by the company making the takeover offer, or perhaps by the governors of the stock exchange). The news will be released to the press and public, and then the shares of both companies will again be opened for trading. You'll receive an indication from management as to whether or not it thinks the takeover bid is a good idea and in the best corporate interest.

The bid for the shares of the company is always higher than their market price when the announcement is made. Obviously, a takeover bid is very positive news for you: another company thinks so highly of your company that they want to buy it. You will receive direct word on a takeover bid, in the form of notification in the mail, a call from your broker, and probably a call from the brokerage firm hired to handle the takeover. You may be offered cash, bonds, shares, or a combination of these for the shares you currently hold.

What should you do? Decide whether or not you wish to tender (agree to sell) your shares to the takeover bidder. You can also choose to sell in the marketplace and not get caught up in this activity, just taking the money immediately and going on to another investment, thanking your good fortune. (You will pay commission if you sell your shares in the market whereas you won't if you tender your shares to the company bidding for them. You can go through your own broker in either case.)

You can also hold onto your shares, believing that now a bid has been made other suitors may show up offering a higher price. You could become involved in a bidding war.

Suddenly you will see lots of action. Takeover terms will be fired like bullets. You may hear "hostile takeover" (one in which management does not approve), or "white knight" (a different takeover bid by a rescuer company that management likes better than the first bidder) or "greenmail" (when someone is pretending to be involved in a takeover just to have the shares go up in price so that he or she can make a profit). By the way, true greenmail is not permitted under Ontario securities law.

Takeovers can take time so if you are in a hurry, the best strategy is selling in the market, paying the commission, and moving on. You should be ecstatic because you made a wise investment decision and now you've been rewarded. Congratulations.

What happens if you do not react to a takeover bid by selling your shares in the market or tendering them to the bidder. Maybe nothing — after all, the takeover attempt may fail. But if 90% of shares are tendered for a takeover bid, applicable corporate law usually states that all remaining shares can be "forced in" for purchase by the bidder in something resembling expropriation.

If there is activity in a company whose shares you hold, activity that you have trouble understanding, you don't have to wait for the broker's call. Call your broker yourself to find out what is going on. Unlike you, your broker may be in touch with the situation and may be comfortable with what seems to you to be unusual activity. But for your own financial comfort, always take action to protect and understand your interests.

WHAT IF MY DIVIDEND IS CUT?

Let's say you own 100 shares of Q Company and it just cut its dividend for the quarter. What now?

First of all, understand why the company is doing this. It is attempting to preserve capital. So perhaps there is a problem with the cash flow.

For any company experiencing cash flow problems, a first line of defence is to cut expenses. This may mean cutting the common share dividend, and in extreme cases it means cutting the preferred share dividend, as we discussed in Chapter Seven. By cutting the dividend, the company is clearly signalling that it is not in great financial shape. You need to pause to review your investment strategy. Think of the reasons you bought the shares in the first place. Determine what the company's problem appears to be and what action you should take. Get some idea of whether the problem is very temporary, short term, long range, or of uncertain duration.

As Gerald M. Loeb says in *The Battle for Investment Survival,*
> Writing down your cogent reasons for making an investment — what you expect to make, what you expect to risk, the reasons why — should save you many a dollar. . . . It also gives you tangible material to evaluate the whys and wherefores of your profits or losses.

By the time the dividend is cut, professional investors will have suspected problems and taken action, so the stock price will probably have already declined. There will have been some signals beforehand: possibly declining earnings, cancelled contracts, tariffs, tax increases, product failure, court cases with the ruling against the company, or a poor economic outlook for the entire industry. Any number of factors can contribute to a decline in fortunes and the cutting of the dividend. Watch for these early warning signals.

Faced with the facts, you may want to sell. Another possibility is to buy more shares because the price is low and you have faith in the company and its ability to recover. This strategy, which is known as *averaging down* (you buy more shares at a lower price, which reduces your average cost), involves increased risk, so weigh the facts, risk, and reward carefully before proceeding. (This action would be taken by a high-risk investor, never by an ultra-conservative one.)

Only you can make this decision and only on each individual case. There is no formula. But you must face the facts squarely. Then you must estimate the risk to your capital of staying in or of buying more. You must calculate the reward that you expect, and you should put a time limit on your projections so that you can calmly keep tabs on the situation and make other alterations as and if necessary.

Use the best/worst case analysis here. Is the situation temporary? Is it really a long-term opportunity to buy more shares? Also, try to assess realistically whether you have made a mistake. It happens to everyone. If you have, maybe it is better to sell and drive on.

HOW CAN I TELL WHEN A STOCK PRICE IS AT ROCK BOTTOM?

MY RECOMMENDED STRATEGY: If bad news is still coming out about a company, but the share price is not declining further, you are getting a signal that the share price has levelled off and the worst may be over. So start paying close attention. Current fundamental analysis of the company may not show any improvements, but there are a variety of ways of approaching an investment decision. You may find you are more impressed with management's ability to handle the crisis facing the company, than with the short-term problems it is suffering from.

I knew a broker who used to comb the annual report racks. He said that once a company stopped issuing a glossy annual report, he knew that it had taken its costs in hand. He loved to find annual reports on plain paper with black and white photographs. An inexpensively made annual report provided him with an important indicator of the management of the company.

Recall the discussion of the contrarian approach from the last chapter. This may be a time to try it. Consider buying a stock that has temporarily fallen on hard times and holding it until it recovers.

But be careful! Don't be a Don Quixote, charging ahead and ignoring evidence. You may feel that you are right and others are wrong and that the price has declined so much that it can't go any lower. Do you want to bet? You must be able to face up to all the facts and then make a business decision.

If you choose to buy, it's important to set a time frame. Look at the company's prospects and consider what might happen, in six months, in nine months, or in a year. You must balance the risk against the reward that might be available. One thing is certain: there is less room for the price to fall when a company's stock has declined substantially.

Another way of assessing value is to look at the break-up value of the company. It is calculated by subtracting the firm's liabilities from its assets and dividing this by the number of common shares. (Luckily, analysts often do this for you.) The question you are asking is this: if the company sold everything it owned and paid off its debts, what would be your portion on a per share basis?

In the case of Pacific Western Airlines, the shares declined in price when airline deregulation was announced. However, people forgot that the break-up value came to more than $20 per share. On the advice of my broker friend, Naomi Ridout, I examined this company and made a lot of money for clients by purchasing these shares for them. Ultimately the stock recovered substantially (see Exhibit 12.2).

EXHIBIT 12.2
Pacific Western Airlines Stock Chart

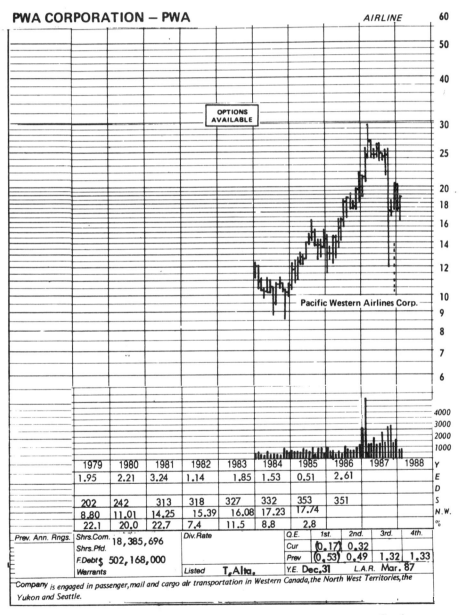

Graphoscope

Keep in mind that you never know for sure when a stock has hit its low. No one rings a bell, and only fools and liars say they can pick the bottom price. You must decide what represents good value to you. Back to Bernard Baruch, who recommends in his autobiography, "Don't try to buy at the bottom and sell at the top. This can't be done — except by liars."

MY SHARES AREN'T TRADING — WHAT'S HAPPENING?

When a company's shares exhibit unusual trading activity, a stock exchange can stop the trading in them, with or without the company's request. The rationale for the halt-trading order, as it is known, is that everyone should be able to get information at the same time. The regulators watch trading patterns closely, and heavy trading volume may be a clue that some information has leaked out. Stock can be halted for half an hour for a press release or longer, depending on the circumstances. Sometimes it is halted permanently because the company has declared insolvency.

An exchange can also halt a stock when a company has not met its listing requirements, such as timely filing of annual reports and quarterly statements.

When stock is halted you cannot buy or sell. Call your broker to find out what is suspected and then wait for the announcement. Being patient is the only action you can take at this point.

BUYING IS EASY BUT HOW DO I KNOW WHEN TO SELL?

Knowing when to sell is tough. When making a sell decision, people feel they are putting their investment acumen on the line. It's a natural instinct to want to do the best, and every investor buying for potential growth wants to sell at the top. You can only try your best and sell an investment when you've found another one which you like better.

An intelligent investor does not have to be a market genius. He or she is content to know when to take a profit and doesn't lie awake at night regretting anything. Light profits make heavy purses, and you'll never go broke taking a profit are two bits of stock market wisdom.

Consider these two examples. A man, the client of a broker I know, bought a stock at $20. The stock went to $30, and his broker recommended selling based on the client's objectives. He had made 50% on his money, which was his investment goal. He sold. The next week, the stock went to $40, and the client was furious.

While it is natural to feel some regret in this situation, it helps to remember that no one knows the future. The best guidelines we can work with are your personal objectives and goals. For this stock, like any other, the price could have gone down, instead of continuing to climb. It is only in hindsight that the answer is known.

Another example. I know a broker who recommended that his client sell a stock which· had gone from $5 to $8 in a very short time period. The client said no, he wanted to wait for $8.25. The stock went back to $5, and the client was outraged. Greed and fear are powerful market forces which you battle every day. Trying to squeeze out the last 25 cents may not always be wise or possible. Again, constantly review your goals, objectives, and strategy. Price isn't the only clue you receive to sell.

Another smart investing idea is not to look for round numbers when selling: $40 or $50 is what *everybody* wants to sell at.

MY RECOMMENDED STRATEGY: If you are looking to sell at a specific price, put in a limit order at $39¾ or $39⅞, rather than $40, and you'll beat the crowd. Lots of people have the idea of selling at round numbers, such as $40 or $50, so there tends to be a huge supply of stock at such a price. Many times a stock will get right up to the round number but resist staying there. In addition, an aggravating thing tends to happen when a stock goes through a round number: it has a tendency to go up another 10% from that level.

Some days you feel you just can't win. So don't put yourself in a win/lose situation by trying to pick the top prices. If you have an investment objective, you will do better by sticking to it. Don't allow yourself to be blown off course by every change in the volatile market winds. Be consistent.

When you sell, you have made a decision based on the best information you have *today*. Tomorrow could bring something else. If you make money, there is no reason to regret your decision. The only mistake you can make here is not to stick to your objectives when trying to achieve your goals. If you have met your goal, you should be congratulating yourself for meeting your objectives. What benefit can regret provide? None. In fact, it is detrimental to your future decisions because it causes you to focus unproductively on the past. Stick to your objectives, enjoy your profit, and forget the regret. It could have gone either way.

If the stock continues to rise after you sell, it's history. Complaining won't cause you to make more money and no one has a crystal ball. Bernard Baruch, who did pretty well, said that he made all of his money by selling too soon.

MY RECOMMENDED STRATEGY: Part of marketwise investment is setting your upper and lower price targets. You should always give your broker parameters: for example, to get out if the stock drops 20% or if it rises 30%. Keep the lines of communication open, and set objectives before you buy a stock. You can enter limit orders to sell with your broker so that you don't have to make a snap decision. It is hard to maintain perspective if you are caught up in the emotion of the moment, but a wavering decision can wreck your game plan. Selling, even at a loss, may be better than hanging on to a losing proposition. Sometimes it is necessary but it's never pleasant.

SEVEN INVESTING MISTAKES YOU DON'T NEED TO MAKE
Here's a summary of certain pitfalls I've seen tempt unwary investors.

- Constantly changing your mind and being inconsistent, either with your objectives or your securities. Is it gold today, real estate yesterday, and orange juice futures tomorrow? You develop your plan and work within it.

- Panicking and letting your emotions make your investment decisions. This is what you want to avoid. You are making business decisions, so plan and be prepared.

- Blaming others for things which they have no control over — for example, what happens tomorrow. Investing is about making decisions, formulating objectives, assessing risk and reward, and working towards goals. Blaming does not help you with any of these.

- Becoming caught in the greed and fear that drive the market. Investors must control these emotions if they want to be successful. Kenny Rogers sang, "You've got to know when to hold them and know when to fold them." Remember facts, risk, and reward.

- Not paying attention to what is happening to your money and your investments. Other people are your advisors, but you are the decision maker so be on top of your situation and be sure to make the best of your circumstances. Your advisors will act in your best interests but the buck stops with you.

- Hoping problems will go away — and ignoring the facts and advice of experts. Having too great an ego stake in your investments can be very costly. You will be wrong sometimes because *everyone* is wrong sometimes. Just don't let your ego get in the way of making correct business decisions.

- Saying you will sell a stock that has declined only when it returns to the price you paid for it. The expression "cut your losses" comes to mind. In some cases, the stock will never return to what you paid for it. Sell and learn from the experience.

All sorts of things can happen to you as an investor, some of them good, some bad, and some incomprehensible. Keep it all in perspective, and do the best you can under the circumstances with the information you have today.

In this chapter we considered
  — when and how to pay for transactions,
  — what to do with certificates and dividends,
  — Painless Portfolio Building idea 3,
  — stock splits, takeovers, and averaging down,
  — when to buy and when to sell,
  — seven investor mistakes and how to avoid them.

It's now time to fit together everything you've learned up to this point.

Chapter Thirteen

PUTTING IT ALL TOGETHER

What you have been developing as you have been working through this book is an investment sense. It is an understanding of what happens, where it happens, and why. With all of this newly acquired knowledge of what's available, let's return to the Banquet Table and put it all together.

You originally articulated your goals and understood that a strategy of saving or investing is needed if you are going to meet your objectives of regular income, low-risk growth, high-risk growth, and/or tax savings which will bring you closer to achieving your goals.

In Chapter Three we looked at a diagram of goals, strategies, and objectives as they relate to our example of an ultimate goal, buying a house. Now, in Exhibit 13.1, complete the same diagram with one of *your* goals and the steps you'll need to take to reach it.

EXHIBIT 13.1
Reaching Your Ultimate Goal

First strategy: _____

_____

Eventual strategy: _____

_____

You are now here

First goal: _____

_____

Ultimate goal: _____

Remember, only 10% of the population has written articulated goals. In your quest to advance, you must put your goals down on paper and examine the routes you will take to reach them.

Now you know the way to financial freedom through Painless Portfolio Building with Canada Savings Bonds, mutual funds, and dividend reinvestment plans. You are no longer content to be part of the crowd with your investments; you want to leapfrog ahead.

There are many ways to put your money to work for you. The investment ideas in this book are simply thought-starters. You have a wide variety of choices of instruments, of companies, and of countries to consider investing in. As I said earlier, investment is now possible almost anywhere in the world where shares are traded. It really is a global marketplace.

Your personal investment program will follow your master plan of strategies for accumulating funds and investing them. Having recorded where you now spend your money, you can determine if you want to redirect some of it to reach your investment objectives. You know that a stockbroker can help you formulate a plan designed to move you towards meeting your objectives, but you must never forget that what you are dealing with is *your* money.

Regardless of your circumstances, tap your resources. Be creative. Work towards the things you want to accomplish in life — financial freedom is one of those things. Keep referring to the items you have written in this book. Review how far you have come in the last five years. Five years from now, complete the questionnaire again; I'm sure you'll be pleasantly surprised. If you develop a keen desire to accomplish your goals, you are well on the way to reaching them.

You are going to make mistakes because everyone does. You know that. I hope that this book has alerted you to some errors so that you can save money by knowing what not to do, as well as what you should do. Every single investment style has its risks, be they inflation, taxation, or possible losses of capital. You must assess the facts, risks, and potential rewards before you take action.

After people gain additional information, they sometimes look back at "dumb" decisions. I know I do. But each decision contributes to your knowledge, which means you'll be that much better the next time.

The business world operates in cycles. So does the economy. It expands and it contracts. It reaches peaks and it falls into troughs. And then the cycles begin again. Opportunities are available at all of these times, and so are traps. You've seen examples of what kinds of investments have worked under what circumstances and why.

Taxation has contributed greatly to the advancement of investments in the public's eye. With the registered retirement savings plan market now at more than $50 billion, we know that more and more investors are conscious of the need to save tax and to accumulate funds and invest them for their future.

Throughout the book, I have tried to take various investment concepts, such as dollar cost averaging and negative rate of return, and give you concrete examples of how they work.

As I said in the introduction, you will find similar circumstances over and over again in the world of investments. One example is the seesaw reaction of various securities, such as when interest rates rise, preferred shares with fixed-rate dividends fall in order to remain competitive in the marketplace. Another is the idea of premiums, be they for bonds, convertible preferred shares, or the exercise price of warrants. I know that now you've read this book, you'll start saying to yourself, "Yes, that reminds me of . . ." Lo and behold, you have your first basis for comparison.

The amount of information available to you is phenomenal, but never let it intimidate you.

You know that what suits you may be totally unsuitable for your next-door neighbour, and that's great. It would be a shame to have this wide variety of investment choices but everyone wanting just one of them. Diversification across more than one industry or with more than one investment is your aim when you are building your portfolio. Remember the asset mix of cash, bonds, and stocks, too.

Overall, this book exists to give you tools you can use in the investment world. It's sort of a starter kit to use as your base for exploring particular areas of investment that interest you.

As a marketwise investor, you will make the best of your circumstances whatever they may be. Bennett Goodspeed says in *The Tao Jones Averages*: "The first enemy is fear. If a man runs away out of fear and avoids investing, nothing will happen except that he will never learn. Though you can read many books about the theory of investing, you can never learn unless you become a player."

This takes us back to our discussion of theory and reality. I hope that through the examples and stories in this book I have shown you what actually can happen to certain investments under specific circumstances. Try to avoid the pitfalls, know your goals, work towards meeting your objectives, and good luck.

> *No one knows what he can do until he tries.*
> — Publilius Syrus

BIBLIOGRAPHY

Baruch, Bernard. *My Own Story*. New York: Holt, Rinehart and Winston, 1957.

Bernstein, Jacob. *Investor's Quotient: The Psychology of Successful Investing in Commodities & Stock*. New York: Wiley, 1980.

Bolles, Richard Nelson. *What Color Is Your Parachute?* Berkeley, CA: Ten Speed Press, 1984 rev. 1986, 1987, 1988.

Canadian Securities Institute. *Investment Terms & Definitions*. Toronto: CSI.

——— *How to Invest in Canadian Securities*. Toronto: CSI.

——— *Canadian Mutual Funds*. Toronto: CSI.

——— *Manual for Registered Representatives*. Toronto: CSI.

Delaney, Tom. *The Delaney Report on RRSPs*. Toronto: McGraw-Hill Ryerson, annual.

Dines, James. *How the Average Investor Can Use Technical Analysis for Stock Profits*. Dines Chart Corporation, 1972.

Dreman, David. *New Contrarian Investment Strategy: The Psychology of Stock Market Success*. New York: Random House, 1983.

Edwards, Robert D., and Magee, John. *Technical Analysis of Stock Trends*. Springfield, MA: John Magee, 1948.

Gluskin, Alexander M. *Confessions of an Options Strategist*. Toronto: Hounslow Press, 1985.

Goodspeed, Bennett W. *The Tao Jones Averages: A Guide to Whole-Brained Investing*. New York: E.P. Dutton, 1983, Penguin Books, 1984.

Hatch, Dr. James and White, Dr. Robert. *Canadian Stocks, Bonds, Bills and Inflation*. Virginia: Financial Analysts Research Foundation, 1988.

Homer, Sidney, and Liebowitz, Martin L., *Inside the Yield Book: Tools for Bond Market Strategy*. New York: Prentice-Hall, 1973.

Huff, Darrell and Geis, Irving. *How to Lie With Statistics*. New York: Norton, 1954.

Fosback, Norman G. *Stock Market Logic: A Sophisticated Approach to Profits on Wall Street*. New York: Econometric, 1986.

Kelman, Steven G. *Mutual Fund Advisor*. Financial Times of Canada, 1987.

Loeb, Gerald M. *Battle for Investment Survival*. New York: Simon & Schuster, 1965.

Louis, David. *Tax-Saving Strategies for the Canadian Investor*. Toronto: Hume Publishing.

Louis, David. *RRSP Strategies*. Toronto: Hume Publishing.

MacKay, Charles. *Extraordinary Popular Delusions and the Madness of Crowds*. Templeton Publications, 1985.

McMillan, Lawrence. *Options as a Strategic Investment*. New York: New York Institute of Finance, 1980.

Maltz, Dr. Maxwell. *Psycho-Cybernetics: A New Way to Get More Living Out of Life*. New York: Simon & Schuster, 1983.

Naisbitt, John. *Megatrends: Ten New Directions Transforming Our Lives*. New York: Warner Books, 1983.

Prechter, Robert. *The Elliott Wave Theory*. Gainsville, GA: New Classics Library, 1985.

Robbins, Anthony. *Unlimited Power, The New Science of Personal Achievement*. New York: Simon & Schuster, 1986.

Sheehy, Gail. *Passages*. New York: Bantam Books, Inc., 1977.

Smith, Adam. *The Money Game*. New York: Random House, Inc., 1976.

Templeton, Sir John Marks. "Speech by John M. Templeton to the Canadian Mutual Fund and Investment Dealers and Stock Brokers, Toronto, July 24, 1987."

Toronto Stock Exchange. *Canadian Shareowners: Their Profile and Attitudes*. Toronto: December, 1986.

Train, John. *The Money Masters:* 2nd ed. New York: Harper and Row, 1985.

Waitley, Denis. *Seeds of Greatness*. New York: Pocket Books, 1984.